Nancy Smith & Lynda Milligan

Divide & CONQUER!
Quilt it Your Way

D0534232

☆ ☆ ☆ ☆ ☆
POSSIBILITIES®

...Publishers of DreamSpinners® patterns, I'll Teach
Myself™ sewing products, and Possibilities® books...

Acknowledgements

We would like to dedicate this book to our very good friend, longtime employee, and most valuable (couldn't live without) editor, Sharon Holmes.

About 18 years ago, Sharon wandered into our small store when we were having a sale. It was one of our first sales, and we were rather unsure how to handle it. The store had become swamped with customers. As Sharon and her young son, Alexander (then about three years old), entered, one of us asked, "How would you like to work a while?" She parked her son under a table and began cutting fabric. Six hours later she took a long, deep breath and said, "Wow!" Thus began our wonderful relationship.

Over the years Sharon has always given her very best to us and has accommodated all our learning adventures and misadventures. We all have grown up together. Our knowledge and styles have changed, but she continues to strive for the sense of perfection that she knows is possible. Sharon is an excellent editor, organizer, quilt maker, class schedule writer, quilting teacher, and computer operator, as well as mom, wife, and daughter. Her own daughter is through medical school and into a residency, and her son is a senior in college. What an accomplished lady!

We are so very pleased to have Sharon as a part of our company. We all are extremely proud to dedicate this book to her.

Special Thanks

Jane Dumler, Joanne Malone, Jan Hagan, Ann Petersen, Michielle Schlichenmayer,
Barbara O'Melia, Sharron Shimbel — For stitching & quilting
Carolyn Schmitt, Sandi Fruehling — For long-arm machine quilting
Crate & Barrel Furniture — For photography in their store
Four Mile Historic Park — For photography in their museum
Sharyn Craig — For teaching in our store, Great American Quilt Factory,
and inspiring the North Winds block that was used in Midnight Garden
Sue Nickels — For sharing her method of cutting the batting away from the area she isn't quilting

Credits

Sharon Holmes — Editor, Technical Illustrator
Susan Johnson — Designer, Hand Illustrator, Photo Stylist
Valerie Perrone — Designer, Technical & Hand Illustrator
Lexie Foster — Cover Designer, Photo Stylist, Hand Illustrator
Sara Tuttle — Designer
Lani Ho'a — Technical Illustrator
Sandi Fruehling — Editorial Assistant
Chris Scott — Copy Reader
Brian Birlauf — Photographer
Lee Milne — Digital Photographer
Judy Turner — Our Method 2 was made popular by her book *Awash with Colour* from That Patchwork Place

POSSIBILITIES®
…Publishers of DreamSpinners® patterns, I'll Teach Myself™ sewing products, and Possibilities® books…

Divide & Conquer
©2000 by Nancy Smith & Lynda Milligan

Published in the United States of America by *Possibilities*®, Denver, Colorado.
Library of Congress Catalog Card Number: 00-108902
ISBN: 1-880972-43-3

Photo Index

APPLIQUE   Our favorite method of applique is the fusible web technique with a buttonhole stitch finish. Patterns are reversed and ready to be traced. Be sure to have plenty of fusible web on hand if using this method. Reverse and add seam allowance to patterns if doing hand applique.

Ideas for
Midnight
Garden
Patterns

3

Why Quilt This Way?

How many times have you found yourself wanting to make a bed quilt only to quickly talk yourself out of it?

The phrases that come to mind are:

"I only have one life, and I want to do things other than make just one quilt in that lifetime."

"I could never do anything that huge."

"It's just too heavy."

"My back and shoulders could never handle machine quilting something of that size."

"I could never squeeze something so large through that little space on my sewing machine."

"I can't afford to pay someone to quilt all of the tops I get finished."

There must be a hundred other comments that would seem just as appropriate regarding machine quilting—or for that matter, hand quilting—a quilt large enough to accommodate a queen or king bed.

When we first started quilting over twenty years ago, there was a popular technique called "quilt-as-you-go". The concept seemed wonderful, and we, as well as many of our friends, did our share of experimenting with this technique. The main thrust of this concept was to make blocks, then assemble them separately with backing and batting, and then quilt them. When you were completely finished with the stack of blocks, you began the assembly process. That is where the real work began. In our minds—and in the minds of our friends—we only had to do one of these "quilt-as-you-go" quilts, and that was enough! The small squares were nice to work on and were very portable, but stitching all of the blocks together became incredibly laborious. Most

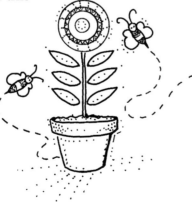

of the people we know discontinued using the process many years ago.

Here we are today on the cusp of the twenty-first century. Quilting is as popular as ever. It has become a passion for many people as a way to relax and reduce stress. New products, techniques, battings, sewing machines, and other technological advances are impacting today's quilters. Because of these changes, we are now able to revisit the idea of "quilt-as-you-go". However, we call it **Divide and Conquer: Quilt It Your Way**. You can make large quilts—even extra super-duper large quilts—by breaking them down into manageable pieces. It is almost like magic when your queen or king quilt is finished!

We use four methods to *Divide and Conquer* these large quilts. In Method 1, a quilt top is pieced and quilted in manageable sections before being joined together. In Method 2, individual blocks are quilted before being zigzagged  together edge to edge and then joined. Strips cover the seams and add a unique design element. Method 3 employs a technique in which the top is made whole but the batting is split into sections which reduces the bulk for quilting. In Method 4, the center section of a quilt is quilted, then borders are added and quilted.

How is this book set up?

Our book is set up with thorough directions for each quilt using one of the four *Divide and Conquer* methods. We have given every quilt a specific size, a yardage chart, and a cutting chart. Following those are full directions for making it in one of the four techniques. We show you how to break your quilt down into manageable units so that each unit can be either hand or machine quilted with ease. These are not necessarily individual blocks that are being quilted, but halves, thirds, or other sections of a quilt. It is more like quilting a wall hanging or a baby quilt. The projects become smaller for manipulating through the small opening of the sewing machine or for carrying around to hand quilt. The quilt sections also weigh less and so are easier to maneuver.

Because this book is set up in a traditional manner, it's also easily adaptable to using the directions for making the quilt top in one piece and quilting it as a whole unit. Many people have long-arm quilting machines, and that method of quilting is perfect for these large quilts.

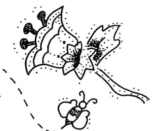

The four *Divide and Conquer* techniques are interchangeable. You may prefer one of the methods over the others and want to adapt the quilt you like best in the book to one of the other methods. Almost any quilt can be made with Method 1, 3, or 4, and Method 2 has many uses as well. There are so many *Possibilities!*

What materials and tools work best?

Quilting has kept pace with the rest of the world in technological advances and new and improved products. There are many new **battings** on the market. No longer, as in the days of our grand-mothers, do we have to quilt cotton batting every half inch! The cotton and cotton blend battings of today are more dense and more durable, making them ideal for quilting on the sewing machine. They are lump-free and can be quilted much farther apart than the battings of old.

The battings we used for the quilts in this book were the ***flattest*** ones on the market, because of the techniques being used to join sections of quilts. There are many different battings available in this category. We used Soft Touch® by Fairfield (100% cotton), Quilter's Dream Cotton™ (100% cotton—Request and Select lofts), and Hobbs Heirloom® Premium (80% cotton, 20% polyester). All the new cotton and cotton blend battings have their own rate of shrinkage and their own set of rules for prewashing, so be sure to follow the manufacturer's directions for pretreating the batting before using it.

Our yardage charts list the sizes of the batting *pieces* needed for the quilts rather than naming bed-sized battings. Battings from different manufacturers vary a great deal in size and are changed periodically, making it difficult to give accurate batting sizes when the batting is going to be cut up before it is used. Also, you can often use leftover pieces of batting from other projects when making a quilt in this way—another perk!

Another great product on the market these days is temporary **basting spray**. There are several different brands available. They are found at quilting, sewing, and craft stores. Ask friends for their opinions about particular brands, or try what's recommended in the shop you frequent. Look for a colorless, odorless spray. The directions on the can should say that it is a temporary bond, can be easily repositioned, and can be washed out. Also, make sure it will not gum the needle. A little experimenting ahead of time on some scrap fabric will save headaches along the way.

Using **printed fabrics for the backings** of quilts made with our methods is a great help. We encourage you to use prints or "busy" fabrics for the the back rather than plain fabrics, as they camouflage the joining seams. Often you have to look very closely to see where the pieces have been stitched together. Backings for these quilts can be made of different, contrasting or coordi-nating fabrics as well, making it possible to use smaller pieces of fabric you already have on hand. This provides an opportunity to have some fun with very different fabrics and experiment with putting many different patterns together. The backing of your quilt can therefore be unique and one-of-a-kind.

Speed, computerization, and specialization of sewing machines has gone along with new technology. One of the greatest boosts to machine quilting is the introduction of the **even-feed foot or walking foot**. Some machines come equipped with them as standard, while others have to be purchased as an option. Either way they are well worth the money. To purchase one, check with your local sewing machine dealer. The basic theory behind even-feed feet is that they feed all the layers of the quilt through the machine at the same time without scooting the top layer ahead of the others. They work great.

Are you ready for a quilting adventure?

After you read through the following general directions for our four *Divide and Conquer* techniques, you are ready to choose a quilt and have your own *Divide and Conquer* adventure!

Method 1  For joining large quilted sections.

1. Quilt Section A to edge of quilt top. Trim backing and batting of **Section A even with quilt top** along edge to be joined.

2. Quilt Section B to within 2-3″ of edge along side to be joined. Other sides of section B that are not being joined may be quilted to the edge.

3. Trim backing and batting of **Section B ½″ from edge of quilt top** along edge to be joined (½″ extends beyond edge of quilt top).

4. Pin batting and backing of Section B out of the way. Place edge of **quilt top only** of Section B to edge of Section A. Pin seam well, easing in any fullness. Stitch with ¼″ seam allowance.

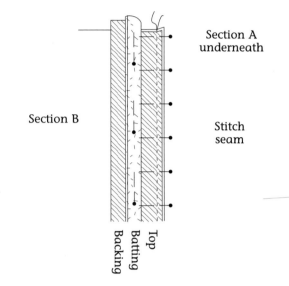

Section A underneath

Section B

Stitch seam

Top
Batting
Backing

5. Press seam toward Section B.

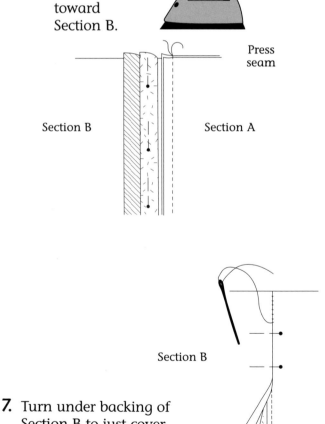

Press seam

Section B   Section A

6. Unpin batting and backing. Trim batting of Section B to meet edge of batting of Section A. Hand whip edges together.

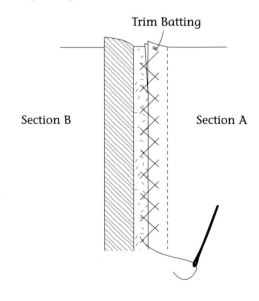

Trim Batting

Section B   Section A

7. Turn under backing of Section B to just cover stitching line and stitch in place by hand.

Turn under backing

8. Finish any remaining quilting along the join.

Method 2

For joining quilted blocks or panels with strips that cover seams.

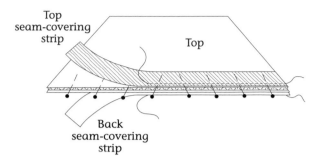

1. Quilt blocks or panels to the edge.

2. Work with one join at a time. Pin seam-covering strips, right sides together, to both sides of one edge of ***one quilted section***. (One strip right side against top and other strip right side against back, all raw edges even.)

3. Stitch through all layers with ¼" seam allowance.

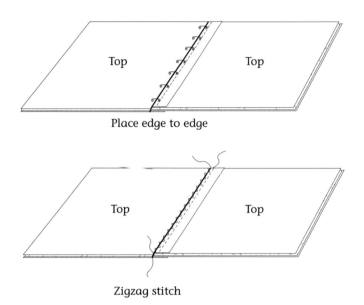

Place edge to edge

Zigzag stitch

4. Lay prepared section **edge to edge** with another section (one with no seam-covering strips) and whip stitch or pin baste with safety pins to hold in place.

5. Stitch sections together with the widest machine zigzag possible. Turn over and zigzag on the other side.

6. On back, fold raw edge of seam-covering strip to meet stitching line. Press. Fold strip over to cover seam and topstitch close to folded edge. Be sure to keep seam-covering strip on top of quilt out of the way when doing this topstitching.

7. On top, turn under just enough seam allowance of seam-covering strip to cover topstitching from Step 6. Hand stitch in place.

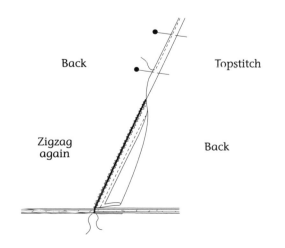

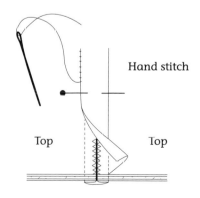

Method 3

For quilting with part of the batting temporarily removed. Diagrams show quilt divided into thirds, but also very effective for dividing smaller quilts in halves.

1. Make quilt top in one piece.

2. Layer backing wrong side up, batting, and quilt top right side up. Pin or spray baste **center third of quilt only**.

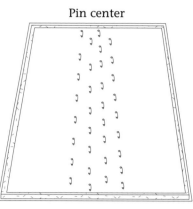

Pin center

3. Fold backing and quilt top away from batting on right side of quilt. Cut batting in a gently curved line close to pins. Curves will make it easy to realign batting. Label batting "top right" and set aside. Repeat on other side of quilt, labeling it "top left".

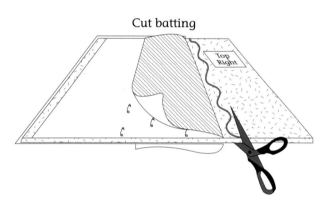

Cut batting

4. Roll up sides to pinned section. Quilt center as desired but stop quilting at least 2″ away from cut edge of batting.

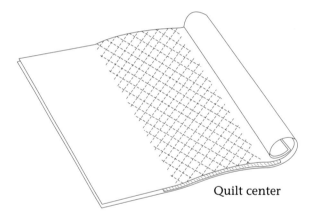

Quilt center

5. At right side of quilt, fold back the quilt top and backing and realign batting edges. Whip stitch curved seam of batting.

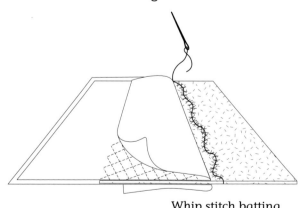

Whip stitch batting

6. Reposition top and backing. Pin or spray baste. Continue quilting.

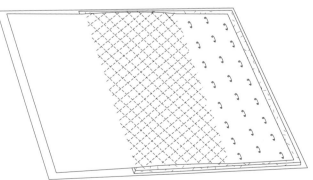

Pin & quilt right side

7. Repeat Steps 5-6 on left side of quilt.

Method 4

For adding borders to quilted center sections.

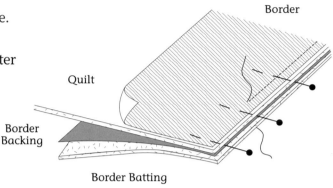

1. Quilt center section of quilt to edge.

2. Trim backing and batting of quilted center section of quilt even with quilt top.

3. Layer
    side border batting
    side border backing, right side up
    quilt center section, right side up
    side border, right side down

4. Stitch through all layers with ¼″ seam allowance. Trim batting out of seam allowance as close to stitching line as possible.

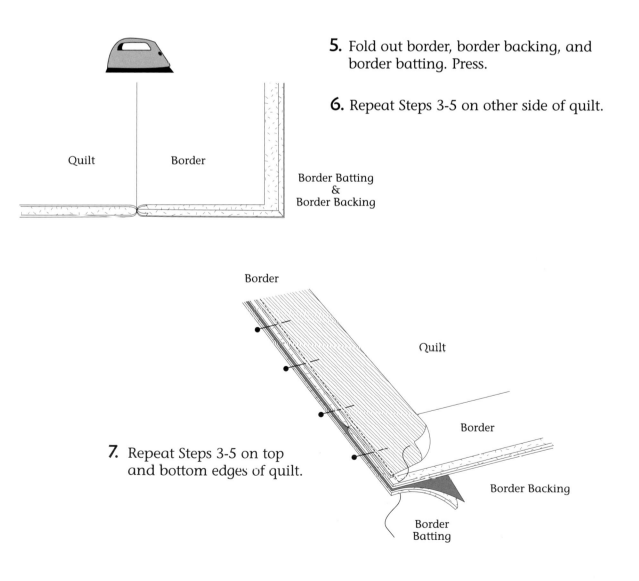

5. Fold out border, border backing, and border batting. Press.

6. Repeat Steps 3-5 on other side of quilt.

7. Repeat Steps 3-5 on top and bottom edges of quilt.

Precious Gems

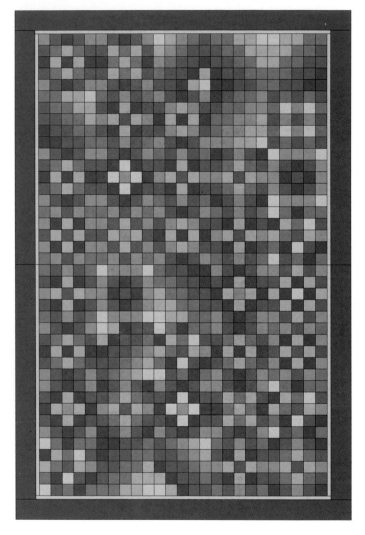

Photo on page 20. Method 1, page 6.

Approximate size 58 x 88″

10″ blocks set 5 x 8

Use 42-45″-wide fabric. When strips appear in the cutting list, cut crossgrain strips (selvage to selvage).

Yardage

Squares – purples, greens
  scraps or quarter-yard pieces to total 4½-5½ yd
Squares – yellows, oranges, pinks
  scraps or eighth-yard pieces to total 1 yd
Border 1   ⅜ yd
Border 2   1⅛ yd
Backing   5⅞ yd
Binding   ¾ yd

Batting – **thin** cotton
  or cotton blend   2 pieces 64 x 50″

Cutting
Squares   2½″ squares – 25 per block
Border 1   7 strips 1¼″ wide
Border 2   8 strips 4″ wide
Binding   8 strips 2½″ wide

Directions

Use ¼″ seam allowance unless otherwise noted.

Please read General Directions, page 4.

1. Cut, lay out, and stitch one block at a time using 2½″ squares. See diagram. Color most blocks to blend into their neighbors, but color some with yellows, oranges, and pinks to make them stand out. Vary the placement of lights and darks from block to block as shown. Make 40 blocks. Press.

2. Stitch blocks together into 8 rows of 5.

3. Stitch top 4 rows together. Press. Stitch bottom 4 rows together. Press.

4. Border 1

   a. Measure length of top section of quilt. Piece strips, if necessary, cut to the measured length, and stitch to sides. Repeat for bottom section of quilt.

   b. Measure width of top section of quilt. Piece strips to the measured length and stitch to top edge. Repeat for bottom section of quilt, stitching border to bottom edge. Press.

5. Border 2: Repeat Step 4.

6. Piece backing to 64″ wide x 100″ long, in 2 vertical panels. Press seam. Cut apart horizontally into 2 pieces 64 x 50″.

7. Layer each quilt section with backing and batting. Pin or spray baste. Quilt as desired, with one restriction: Bottom section may be quilted to the edge, but top section must have 2-3″ left unquilted along the bottom edge for joining.

   Note: Borders may be quilted now or after joining the two sections of the quilt. If quilting now, choose a design that will look okay across the space at the join, or do a meander pattern that can be filled in after the two sections of the quilt are joined.

8. Join the two sections, referring also to General Directions, Method 1, page 6.

   a. Trim batting and backing **even with quilt top on top edge of bottom section of quilt only**.

   b. On **bottom edge of top section** of quilt, trim batting and backing ½" **from edge of quilt top** (½" extends beyond quilt top).

   c. Pin top and bottom sections of quilt together including all three layers of quilt on bottom section and only the quilt top on the top section. Pin well, easing in any fullness. Stitch.

   d. Press seam allowance toward top section of quilt. Fold backing away from batting on top section of quilt and trim batting to just meet edge of batting on bottom section of quilt.

   e. Hand whip edges together.

   f. Turn under backing on top section of quilt to cover stitching line and hand stitch.

9. Finish any remaining quilting at join and in borders.

10. Trim remaining backing and batting even with quilt top.

11. Stitch binding strips end to end. Press in half lengthwise, wrong sides together. Bind quilt using ⅜" seam allowance.

1.

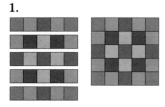

Vary the placement of lights and darks in different blocks

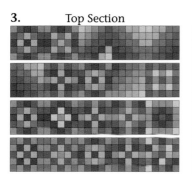

3. Top Section   Bottom Section

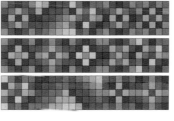

4-5.

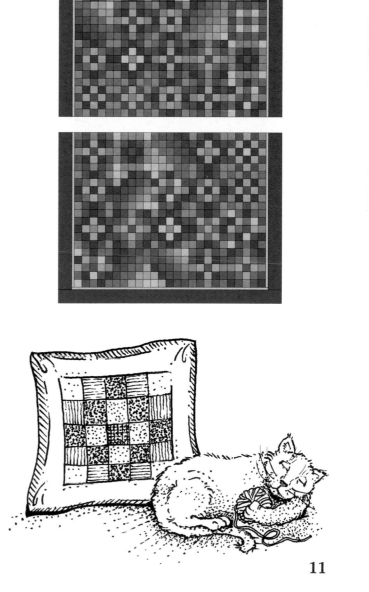

8a. Bottom Section   **8b.** Top Section

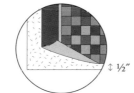

Quilted to edge—
batting & backing
trimmed even with
quilt top

2-3" left unquilted—
batting & backing trimmed
½" from edge of quilt top

Joanne's Sunflowers

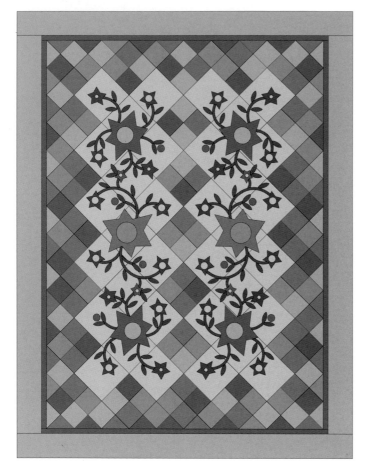

Photo on page 25. Method 3, page 8.

Approximate size 68 x 91″

Use 42-45″-wide fabric. When strips appear in the cutting list, cut crossgrain strips (selvage to selvage).

Yardage

Applique background	2⅜ yd cream
Edging background	⅔ yd ea. of 6 golds/oranges
Appliques – leaves	⅛ yd ea. of 3 greens
vines	¾ yd green
flowers	½ yd ea. of 2 oranges
centers	⅙ yd ea. of 2 reds
Border 1	½ yd
Border 2	1½ yd
Backing	5¾ yd
Binding	¾ yd
Batting – **thin** cotton	
or cotton blend	1 piece 74 x 97″

Cutting Patterns on pages 79-81

Note: Our favorite method of applique is fusible web, and our patterns are set up for it—reversed for tracing and no seam allowances added.

Applique background	34 squares 8½″
Edging background	28 squares 4½″ each fabric
Appliques	see pages 79-81
Border 1	7 strips 1½″ wide
Border 2	8 strips 5½″ wide
Binding	8 strips 2½″ wide

Directions

Use ¼″ seam allowance unless otherwise noted.

Please read General Directions, page 4.

1. Stitch edging background squares into 25 four-patch blocks, 20 side units, and 4 corner units as shown.

2. Lay blocks and units made in Step 1 on floor with applique background squares as shown. Stitch into diagonal rows.

3. Stitch rows together. Press.

4. Trim edges, leaving ¼″ seam allowance as shown. Edge will be bias. Staystitch inside ¼″ seam allowance, if desired.

5. Border 1: Measure length of quilt. Piece side borders to the measured length and stitch to quilt. Press. Measure width of quilt. Piece top and bottom borders to the measured length and stitch to quilt. Press.

6. Border 2: Repeat Step 5.

7. Applique floral motifs. See diagram for order to lay out. Shorten some small vine segments as shown in diagram. Note that right vine motif is a reversed image of left one.

8. Piece backing vertically to same size as batting. Layer backing, batting, and quilt top, but pin or spray baste **only the left section** of the quilt. Fold right side of quilt top and backing away from batting. Carefully cut batting away in a curvy line 3-4″ wide. See General Directions, Method 3, page 8. Attach a label at the top of the quilt saying "top". Attach a label at the top front of the batting piece saying "top right". Set aside.

9. Quilt left side of quilt.

10. Lay quilt on floor, lift right section of quilt top, and replace batting cut from right side, matching curves. Hand whip batting pieces together. Fold quilt top back in position. Pin or spray baste and quilt right side of quilt.

11. Trim batting and backing even with quilt top at outer edges.

12. Stitch binding strips end to end. Press in half lengthwise, wrong sides together. Bind quilt using ⅜″ seam allowance.

1.   Make 25   Side Units Make 20   Corner Units Make 4

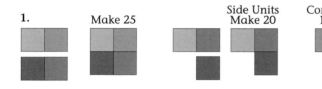

2.

4.   Trim, leaving ¼″ seam allowance

7.   Start with main pieces   Add Small Vine Segments

Large Vine Segment

S-Curve Vine Segment

Large Vine Segment

S-Curve Vine Segment

Then add flowers & leaves

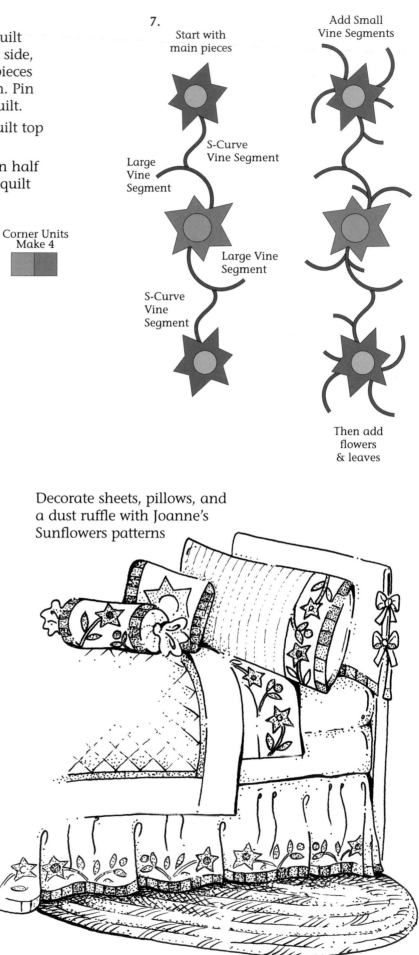

Decorate sheets, pillows, and a dust ruffle with Joanne's Sunflowers patterns

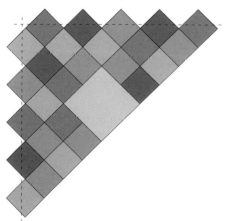

Purely Plum

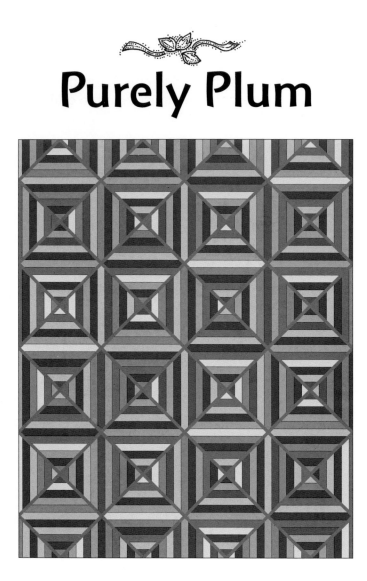

This quilt is reversible.

Photo on page 24. Method 2, page 7.

Approximate size 90x113"

16" blocks set diagonally

Use 42-45"-wide fabric. When strips appear in the cutting list, cut crossgrain strips (selvage to selvage).

Yardage

Blocks	1½ yd each of 13 fabrics
Seam-covering strips	2¾ yd
Backing	10½ yd
Binding	1 yd
Batting – **thin** cotton or cotton blend	40 squares 18"

Cutting

Blocks	18 strips 2½" wide of each fabric
Seam-covering strips	70-76 strips 1¼" wide
Backing	40 squares 18"
Binding	11 strips 2½" wide

Directions

Use ¼" seam allowance unless otherwise noted.

Please read General Directions, page 4.

1. Make 40 blocks:
    a. Lay a piece of batting on the wrong side of a piece of backing. Lay one block strip diagonally across batting, right side up.
    b. Pin another block strip right side down on first strip, matching raw edges. Trim end of strip beyond edge of batting.
    c. Stitch strips together through backing and batting. Fold top strip over and finger press seam.
    d. Repeat to corner using fabrics randomly.
    e. Rotate block 180° and repeat on other side of center strip.
2. Trim blocks to 16" square.
3. Cut 8 blocks into halves and quarters for sides and corners of quilt. See diagram.
4. Lay blocks out on floor, rotating as shown in whole-quilt diagram.
5. Join blocks into diagonal rows, referring also to General Directions, Method 2, page 7.
    a. Work with one join at a time. Pin 1¼" seam-covering strips to both sides of one edge of a quilted square, right sides together, raw edges even. (One strip should be right side down on the top of the square, and the other should be right side against the quilt backing, all raw edges even.) Stitch through all layers with ¼" seam allowance.
    b. Lay square with seam-covering strips *edge to edge* with a square without strips and stitch together with widest zigzag possible. Turn over and zigzag on other side. Continue joining blocks in each row in this way.
    c. On back of each row of blocks, turn under raw edge of each seam-covering strip to meet stitching line. Press. Fold strip over to cover seam. Topstitch close to fold.

d. On front of each row, turn under just enough seam allowance of each seam-covering strip to cover topstitching from Step c and hand stitch in place.

6. Stitch enough seam-covering strips together end to end for each set of rows to be joined.

Join rows together using method in Step 5, making sure seam-covering strips line up from row to row.

7. Stitch binding strips end to end. Press in half lengthwise, wrong sides together. Bind quilt using ⅜″ seam allowance.

1.

Make 40

2.

Trim to 16″

3.

Cut 4 Blocks   Cut 3 Blocks   Cut 1 Block

4.

5a.

Front

Back

5b.

5b.

6.

Mad for Plaid Topper

Photo on page 17

Approximate size 28x73″

Use 42-45″-wide fabric. When strips appear in the cutting list, cut crossgrain strips (selvage to selvage).

Yardage

Background	2⅛ yd blue plaid
Appliques	¾ yd black
Border	⅙ yd each of 7-10 plaids
Backing	2⅜ yd
Binding	⅝ yd
Batting – **thin** cotton or cotton blend	1 piece 34x79″

Cutting Patterns on pages 82-86

Note: Our favorite method of applique is fusible web, and our patterns are set up for it—reversed for tracing and no seam allowances added.

Background	23½ x 68½″
Appliques	see pages 82-86
Border	1 strip 3″ wide from each fabric
Binding	6 strips 2½″ wide

Directions

Use ¼″ seam allowance unless otherwise noted.

1. Cut border strips into rectangles of various lengths—from 5″ to 14″.

2. Stitch rectangles into 2 borders 28½″ long and 2 borders 68½″ long, trimming ends as needed.

3. Stitch long borders to top and bottom of background piece. Stitch short borders to ends. Press.

4. Applique forest to background.

5. Cut backing to same size as batting. Layer and quilt using your favorite methods. Trim batting and backing even with quilt top.

6. Stitch binding strips end to end. Press in half lengthwise, wrong sides together. Bind quilt using ⅜″ seam allowance.

Mad for Plaid, page 18   Mad for Plaid Topper, page 16   **17**

Mad for Plaid

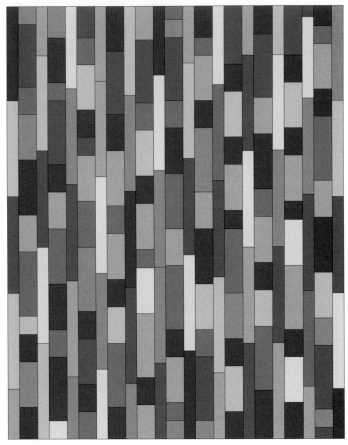

Photo on page 17. Method 1, page 6.

Approximate size 74x96″

Use 42-45″-wide fabric. When strips appear in the cutting list, cut crossgrain strips (selvage to selvage).

Yardage

Strips	⅓ yd each of 35 fabrics
Backing	8⅞ yd
Binding	¾ yd
Batting – **thin** cotton or cotton blend	3 pieces 36x102″

Cutting

Strips	30 strips 3″ wide
	35 strips 4½″ wide
Backing	3 pieces 36x102″
Binding	9 strips 2½″ wide

Directions

Use ¼″ seam allowance unless otherwise noted.

Please read General Directions, page 4.

1. Cut 3″ strips in half, to approximately 3x22″. Stitch all strips together end to end. Press.

2. Cut 4½″-wide strips into random lengths from 5″ to 12″. Stitch strips end to end, making 11 units that are each at least 100″ long. Press. Arrange units on floor, separating colors, staggering seams, and leaving room for 3″ units to be placed between them.

3. Place 3″ units between the 4½″ units, separating colors, staggering seams, and trimming to 100″ long. Also place 3″ strips at left and right sides of quilt top. Trim all 4½″ strips to 100″ long. Do not stitch units together.

4. Spray baste batting pieces to wrong side of backing pieces. Draw a line vertically down center of each piece of batting with a permanent pen or water erasable marker.

5. Center section of quilt: On one piece of batting, lay one 4½″ strip right side up, to left of drawn line. Pin one 3″ strip, right sides together, raw edges even with right edge of 4½″ strip. Stitch through all layers. Fold over to right side and press. Repeat with 4½″ strip; repeat with 3″ strip. Turn piece 180° and add 3″, 4½″, and 3″ strips. Section should have 7 strips, beginning and ending with 3″ strips.

6. Left section of quilt: Repeat Step 5 with one exception—add one more 4½″ strip to right edge. Section should have 8 strips, beginning with 3″ at left and ending with 4½″ at right. See diagram.

7. Right section of quilt: Start by placing a 3″ strip to left of center line, add 4½″, 3″, 4½″, and 3″ strips to right and 4½″, 3″, and 4½″ strips to left. Section should have 8 strips, beginning with 4½″ at left and ending with 3″ at right. See diagram.

8. Join the 3 sections

   a. Trim batting and backing of **left and right edges of center section ½″ from edge of quilt top** (½″ extends beyond quilt top).

b. At right edge of left section and left edge of right section, machine baste last strip of quilt top to backing and batting using an even-feed foot. Trim batting and backing **even with last strip**.

c. Pin left section to center section including all three layers of quilt on left section and only the quilt top on the center section. Stitch. Press seam toward center section of quilt. See General Directions, Method 1, page 6.

d. Fold backing away from batting on center section and trim batting to just meet edge of batting of left section of quilt.

e. Hand whip edges together.

f. Turn under backing on center section to cover stitching line and hand stitch.

g. Repeat Steps c-f for joining right section of quilt to center section.

9. Trim batting and backing at sides of quilt even with quilt top. Trim top and bottom of quilt, making quilt approximately 96″ long.

10. Stitch binding strips end to end. Press in half lengthwise, wrong sides together. Bind quilt using ⅜″ seam allowance.

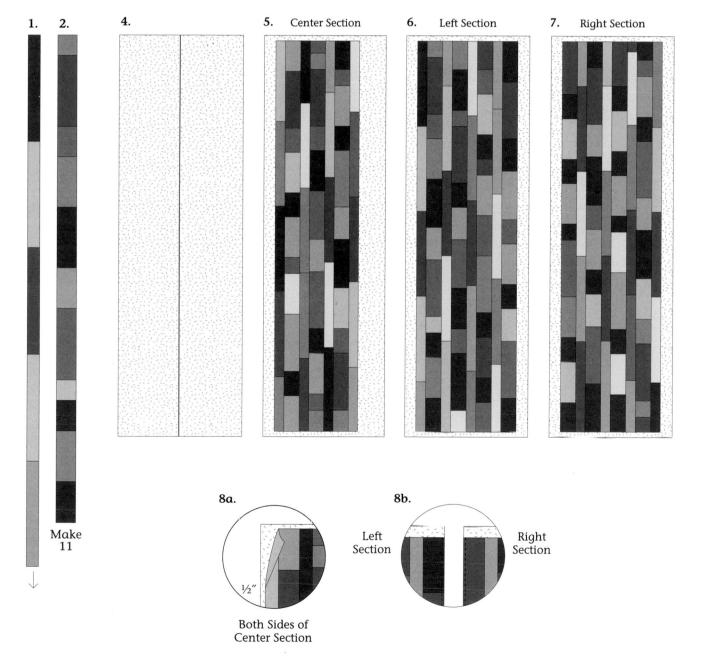

1. 2.

Make 11

4.

5.   Center Section

6.   Left Section

7.   Right Section

8a.

½″

Both Sides of Center Section

8b.

Left Section

Right Section

Cat Nap

Photo on page 28. Method 4, page 9.

Approximate size 51x66″

Use 42-45″-wide fabric. When strips appear in the cutting list, cut crossgrain strips (selvage to selvage).

Yardage

Background & corners	¾ yd each of 6-8 fabrics
Novelty print	optional
Appliques – cat	½ yd
feathers	¼ yd each of 2-3 fabrics
Border 1	½ yd
Border 2	¾ yd
Backing – quilt center	3 yd
Backing – borders	1 yd contrasting fabric
Binding	⅝ yd
Batting – **thin** cotton	
or cotton blend	1 piece 47x62″
	2 pieces 5x58½″
	2 pieces 5x52½″

Cutting Patterns on pages 76-78

Note: Our favorite method of applique is fusible web, and our patterns are set up for it—reversed for tracing and no seam allowances added.

Background	8 strips 3½″ wide
	16 strips 1½″ wide
	28 strips 2½″ wide
	4 squares 3½″ for corners
Appliques	see pages 76-78
Border 1	6 strips 1½″ wide
	4 rectangles 1½x3½″
Border 2	6 strips 3½″ wide
Backing	1 piece 47″ x width of fabric
	1 piece 47x23″
Border backing	6 strips 5″ wide
Binding	6-7 strips 2½″ wide

Directions

Use ¼″ seam allowance unless otherwise noted.

Please read General Directions, page 4.

1. Piece background strips to 62″ long, mixing fabrics, if desired. There is extra yardage so you can vary the number and width from the ones given in the cutting chart. Make at least 4 of the strips 3½″ wide. We pieced sections of a novelty print into different places in some of our strips.

2. Stitch first two pieces of backing in cutting list into a rectangle 47x62″. Place 47x62″ batting piece on wrong side of backing. Basting spray works well for holding the layers together.

3. Set two 3½″ strips aside to use at edges. Using a permanent pen or water erasable marker , lightly mark a straight vertical line down center of batting. Lay one 62″ strip down center of batting on line, right side up. Lay another strip right side down on the first one, matching raw edges on right side. Pin. Using an even-feed foot, stitch through all layers ¼″ from raw edges along right side. Fold strip over and press seam. Repeat to within 3″ of right side of backing and batting. Then finish with a 3½″ strip. Turn quilt 180° and repeat for left side. Trim quilt to 43½x58½″.

4. Add Border 1 at sides of quilt, referring also to General Directions, Method 4, page 9.

   a. Stitch Border 1 strips into 2 pieces 58½″ long. Stitch border backing strips into 2 pieces 5x58½″.

   b. Layer and pin, raw edges even:

      5x58½″ piece of batting
      5x58½″ border backing, right side up
      Right edge of quilt, right side up
      Border 1, right side down

   c. Stitch. Trim batting out of seam allowance as close to stitching line as possible. Fold Border 1, backing, and batting out away from quilt and press seam lightly on both front and back.

   d. Repeat at left edge of quilt.

5. Add Border 2 at sides of quilt.

   a. Stitch Border 2 strips into 2 pieces 58½″ long.

   b. On right side of quilt, pin Border 2, right sides together, raw edges even, to Border 1 through backing and batting. Stitch through all layers. Fold border over and press lightly.

   c. Repeat at left edge of quilt.

6. Add Border 1 at top and bottom of quilt.

   a. Stitch Border 1 strips into 2 pieces 51½″ long. Stitch border backing strips into 2 pieces 5x52½″.

   b. Layer and pin, raw edges even:

      5x52½″ piece of batting
      5x52½″ border backing, right side up
      Top edge of quilt, right side up
      51½″ Border 1, right side down, ends even with Border 2 pieces added to sides in Step 5b

   c. Stitch. Trim batting out of seam allowance as close to stitching line as possible. Fold Border 1, backing, and batting out away from quilt and press seam lightly on both front and back.

   d. Repeat at bottom edge of quilt.

7. Add Border 2 at top and bottom of quilt.

   a. Make 2 Border 2 pieces as shown in diagram, each using corner squares (3½″), Border 1 fabric rectangles (1½x3½″), and Border 2 strips pieced to 3½x43½″.

Continued on page 77.

3.

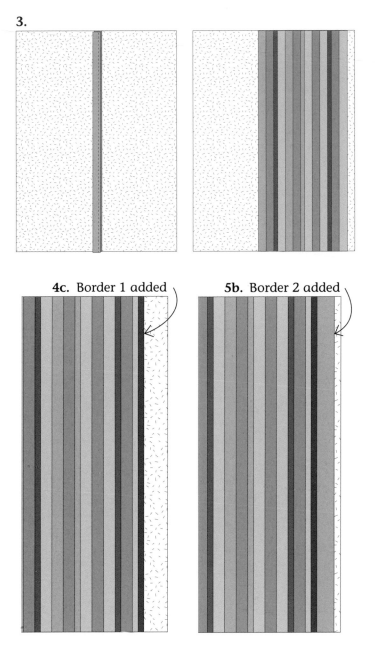

4c. Border 1 added   5b. Border 2 added

6c. Border 1 added

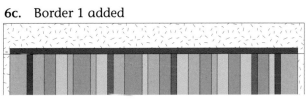

7a. Border 2

7b. Border 2 added

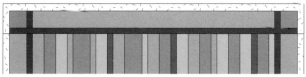

23

Back of Quilt

Squares Askew

Photo on page 21. Method 1, page 6.

Approximate size 65x83″

9″ blocks set 6x8

Use 42-45″-wide fabric. When strips appear in the cutting list, cut crossgrain strips (selvage to selvage).

Yardage

Center squares	⅛ yd each of 4-7 reds, oranges, & pinks
Tilted squares	2¼ yd black print
Block backgrounds	⅙ yd each of 16 blues, greens, & purples
Border 1	⅓ yd
Border 2	1½ yd
Backing	5¾ yd
Binding	¾ yd
Batting – **thin** cotton or cotton blend	2 pieces 71x48″

Cutting

Center squares	48 squares 2½″
Tilted squares	96 rectangles 4¼x6⅝″
Block backgrounds	96 rectangles 4¼x6⅝″
Border 1	7 strips 1¼″ wide
Border 2	8 strips 5½″ wide
Binding	8 strips 2½″ wide

Directions

Use ¼″ seam allowance unless otherwise noted.

Please read General Directions, page 4.

1. Make 24 Block A and 24 Block B, as shown. Hint: For accurate stitching of triangle units, mark seam intersections on wrong side of each triangle and pin through them when stitching one triangle to another.

2. Stitch blocks together into 8 rows of 6, rotating as shown.

3. Stitch top 4 rows together. Press. Stitch bottom 4 rows together. Press.

4. Border 1

   a. Measure length of top section of quilt. Cut strips to the measured length and stitch to sides. Repeat for bottom section of quilt.

   b. Measure width of top section of quilt. Piece strips to the measured length and stitch to top edge. Press. Repeat for bottom section of quilt, stitching border to bottom edge. Press.

5. Border 2: Repeat Step 4.

6. Piece backing to 71″ wide x 96″ long, in 2 vertical panels. Press seams. Cut apart horizontally into 2 pieces 71x48″.

7. Layer each quilt section with backing and batting. Pin or spray baste. Quilt as desired, with one restriction: The bottom section may be quilted to the edge, but the top section must have 2-3″ left unquilted along the bottom edge for joining.

   Note: Border can be quilted now or after joining the two sections of the quilt. If quilting now, choose a design that will look okay across the space at the join, or do a meander pattern that can be filled in after the two sections of the quilt are joined.

8. Join the two sections, referring also to General Directions, Method 1, page 6.

   a. Trim batting and backing *even with quilt top on top edge of bottom section of quilt only*.

   b. On *bottom edge of top section* of quilt, trim batting and backing ½″ *from edge of quilt top* (½″ extends beyond quilt top).

   c. Pin top and bottom sections of quilt together including all three layers of quilt on bottom section and only the quilt top on the top section. Pin well, easing in any fullness. Stitch.

   d. Press seam allowance toward top section of quilt. Fold backing away from batting on top section of quilt and trim batting to just meet edge of batting on bottom section of quilt.

   e. Hand whip edges together.

   f. Turn under backing on top section of quilt to cover stitching line and hand stitch.

9. Finish any remaining quilting at join and in borders.

10. Trim remaining backing and batting even with quilt top.

11. Stitch binding strips end to end. Press in half lengthwise, wrong sides together. Bind quilt using ³⁄₈″ seam allowance.

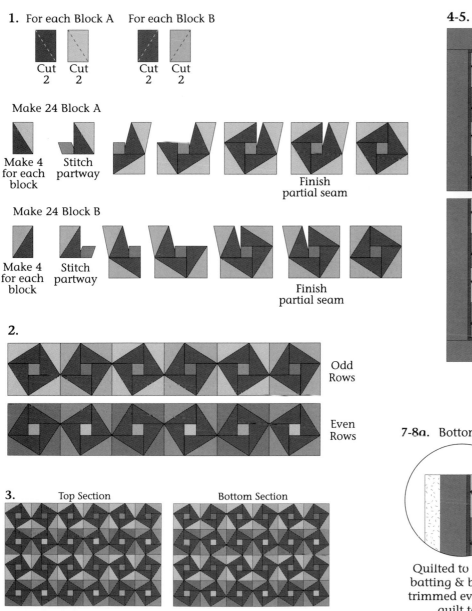

1. For each Block A   For each Block B

Cut 2   Cut 2   Cut 2   Cut 2

Make 24 Block A

Make 4 for each block   Stitch partway   Finish partial seam

Make 24 Block B

Make 4 for each block   Stitch partway   Finish partial seam

2.

Odd Rows

Even Rows

3.   Top Section   Bottom Section

4-5.

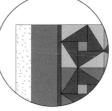

7-8a.   Bottom Section

Quilted to edge–batting & backing trimmed even with quilt top

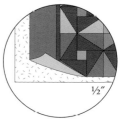

7-8b.   Top Section

½″

2-3″ left unquilted—batting & backing trimmed ½″ from edge of quilt top

Cat Nap, page 22

Front of Quilt

Indigo Braids

Photo on page 52. Method 1, page 6.

Approximate size 66x90″

6″ braid set vertically with applique panels

Use 42-45″-wide fabric. When strips appear in the cutting list, cut crossgrain strips (selvage to selvage).

Yardage

Braids	½ yd each of 12 fabrics
Applique background	2¾ yd
Appliques	¼ yd each of 4-6 greens
	bright scraps to total 2½ yd
	⅝ yd green for vine
Backing	5¾ yd
	(must have 44″ usable width)
Binding	¾ yd
Batting – **thin** cotton or cotton blend	3 pieces 28x96″

Cutting Patterns on pages 73-74

Note: Our favorite method of applique is fusible web, and our patterns are set up for it—reversed for tracing and no seam allowances added.

Braids	340 rectangles 2½x6″
Applique background	4 strips 9½x90½″
	cut on lengthwise grain
Appliques	see pages 73-74
Binding	8 strips 2½″ wide

Directions

Use ¼″ seam allowance unless otherwise noted.

Please read General Directions, page 4.

1. Braids

   a. Make 5 braids as shown, using 68 rectangles in each. Press seam allowances toward point of braid as you go. Press carefully, not allowing braid to stretch.

   b. On wrong side of each long edge of one braid, draw a line ¼″ inside notches between rectangles, as shown. Lines should be 6½″ apart. Staystitch ⅛″ **inside** drawn line. Trim sides of braid on drawn lines. Trim braid to 90½″ long.

   c. Repeat Step b with other braids.

2. Applique

   a. Trace appliques to fusible web.

   b. Fuse to desired fabrics and cut out.

   c. On each 90½″ background strip, lay out 8 vine segments end to end as shown. Arrange flowers and leaves on vine, making sure to cover joins in vine. Fill in gaps with extra leaves and berries. Fuse.

   d. Stitch in place with machine zigzag or buttonhole stitch.

3. Stitch vertical rows of braids and applique together to form three sections of quilt. See diagram. Press seams toward applique panels.

4. Piece backing to 84″ wide x 96″ long, in two vertical panels. Press seams. Cut apart vertically into 3 pieces 28x97″.

5. Layer each section of quilt with batting and backing. Pin or spray baste. Baste closer

together along unsewn edges of braids for extra stability. Quilt as desired with one restriction: All the braids may be quilted to the edge, but the applique rows of the center section of the quilt must have 1-2″ left unquilted along the side edges for joining.

6. Join the three sections, referring also to General Directions, Method 1, page 6.

   a. Trim batting and backing of both long edges of *center section ½″ from edge of quilt top* (½″ extends beyond quilt top).

   b. Trim batting and backing of *right edge of left section and left edge of right section even with quilt top*.

   c. Pin left section to center section including all three layers of quilt on left section and only the quilt top on the center section. Pin well, easing in any fullness. Stitch. Press seam toward center section of quilt.

d. Fold backing away from batting on center section and trim batting to just meet edge of batting of left section of quilt. Hand whip edges together.

e. Turn under backing on center section to cover stitching line and hand stitch. Note: Some extra trimming of the backing may be necessary at this point depending on how close the quilting on the center section is to the join.

f. Repeat Steps c-e for joining right section of quilt to center section.

7. Finish any remaining quilting across the joins.

8. Trim remaining batting and backing even with quilt top.

9. Stitch binding strips end to end. Press in half lengthwise, wrong sides together. Bind quilt using ⅜″ seam allowance.

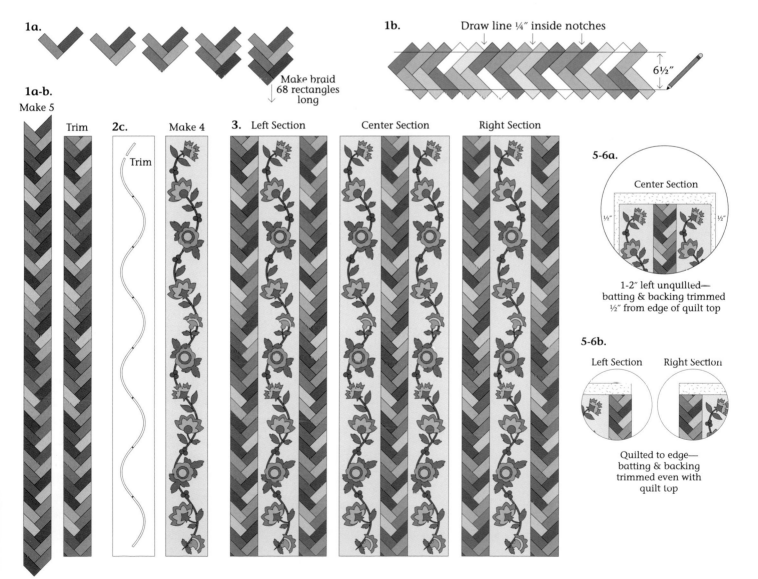

1a.

1a-b.
Make 5

Make braid 68 rectangles long

1b. Draw line ¼″ inside notches

6½″

Trim

2c.
Trim

Make 4

3. Left Section

Center Section

Right Section

5-6a.
Center Section
½″   ½″
1-2″ left unquilted— batting & backing trimmed ½″ from edge of quilt top

5-6b.
Left Section   Right Section
Quilted to edge— batting & backing trimmed even with quilt top

Midnight Garden

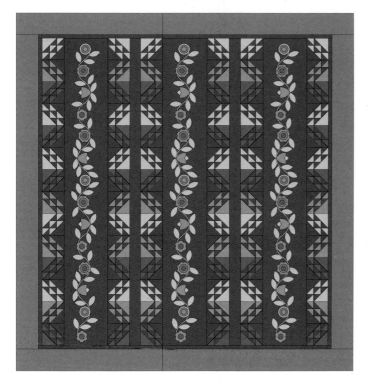

Photo on page 32. Method 1, page 6.

Approximate size 89x98″

6″ block set vertically with applique panels

Use 42-45″-wide fabric. When strips appear in the cutting list, cut crossgrain strips (selvage to selvage).

Yardage

Blocks – black scraps	to total 3¼ yd
bright scraps	to total 3¼ yd
Applique background & sashing strips	2⅝ yd (must have 44″ usable width)
Appliques	⅛ yd each of 8-12 greens bright scraps to total 1½ yd ⅓ yd green for vine
Border 1	½ yd
Border 2	2⅛ yd
Backing	8¾ yd
Binding	⅞ yd
Batting – **thin** cotton or cotton blend	1 piece 45x104″ 1 piece 56x104″

Cutting Patterns on page 75

Note: Our favorite method of applique is fusible web, and our patterns are set up for it—reversed for tracing and no seam allowances added.

Block – for 2 blocks	1 black square 4⅞″
	5 black squares 2⅞″
	1 bright square 4⅞″
	5 bright squares 2⅞″
Applique background	3 strips 11½x84½″ cut on lengthwise grain
Sashing strips	2 strips 3½x84½″ cut on lengthwise grain
Appliques	see page 75
Border 1	9 strips 1½″ wide
Border 2	10 strips 6½″ wide
Binding	10 strips 2½″ wide

Directions

Use ¼″ seam allowance unless otherwise noted.

Please read General Directions, page 4.

1. Cut all squares for blocks in **half** diagonally. Make 84 blocks following diagram on page 34. Press. We used one black and one bright in each block.

2. Stitch blocks into 6 vertical rows, rotating as shown in diagram on page 34.

3. Applique
   a. Trace appliques to fusible web.
   b. Fuse to desired fabrics and cut out.
   c. On each 84½″ applique background, lay out 13 vine segments end to end as shown in diagram on page 34. Arrange flowers and leaves on vine, making sure to cover joins in vine. Fuse.
   d. Stitch in place with machine zigzag or buttonhole stitch.

4. Stitch rows of blocks, rows of applique, and sashing strips together to form two sections of quilt. See diagram on page 35. Sashing strips go between double rows of blocks. Press.

5. Border 1
   a. Measure length of left section of quilt. Piece strips to measured length and stitch

Continued on page 34.

33

Midnight Garden

Continued from page 33.

to left side. Repeat for right section of quilt, stitching border to right side.

b. Measure width of left section of quilt. Piece strips to measured length and stitch to top and bottom edges. Repeat for right section of quilt.

6. Border 2: Repeat Step 5.

7. Piece backing to 101″ wide x 104″ long, in three horizontal panels. Press seams. Cut apart vertically into 2 pieces, 45x104″ and 56x104″.

8. Layer each section of quilt with batting and backing. Pin or spray baste. Quilt as desired with one restriction: The left section of the quilt may be quilted to the edge of the patch-work blocks, but the right section of the quilt must have 1-2″ left unquilted along the edge that will be joined with the left section.

Note: Borders may be quilted now or after joining the two sections of the quilt. If quilting now, choose a design that will look okay across the 1-2″ space at the join, or do a meander pattern that may be filled in after the two sections of the quilt are joined.

9. Join the two sections, referring also to General Directions, Method 1, page 6.

a. Trim batting and backing of *right edge of left section* of quilt *even with quilt top*. Trim batting and backing of *left edge of right section ½″ from edge of quilt top* (½″ extends beyond quilt top).

b. Pin right and left sections of quilt together including all three layers of quilt on left section and only the quilt top on the right section. Pin well, easing in any fullness. Stitch. Press seam toward right section of quilt.

c. Fold backing away from batting on right section and trim batting to just meet edge of batting of left section of quilt. Hand whip edges together.

d. Turn under backing on right section to cover stitching line and hand stitch. Note: Some extra trimming of the backing may be necessary at this point depending on how close the quilting on the right section is to the join.

10. Finish any remaining quilting at join and in borders.

11. Trim remaining batting and backing even with quilt top.

12. Stitch binding strips end to end. Press in half lengthwise, wrong sides together. Bind quilt using ⅜″ seam allowance.

1. For each block

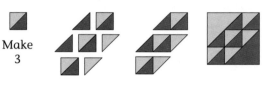

Make 3

2.   3c.

Make 6   Make 3

4-5.   Left Section   Right Section

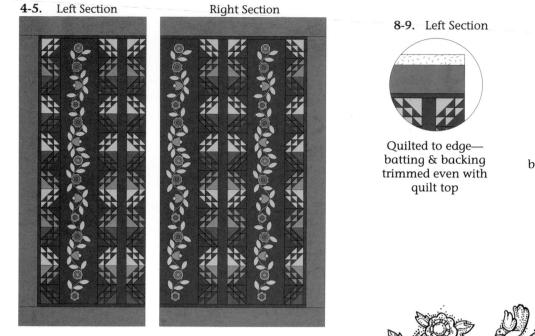

8-9. Left Section

8-9. Left Section   **8-9.** Right Section

Quilted to edge—
batting & backing
trimmed even with
quilt top

1-2″ left unquilted—
batting & backing trimmed
½″ from edge of quilt top

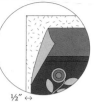

Butterscotch Pudding

Continued from page 37.

6-7.   Top Section

Top Section

9-10.

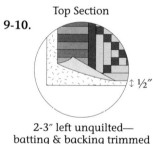

2-3″ left unquilted—
batting & backing trimmed
½″ from edge of quilt top

Bottom Section

Bottom Section

Quilted to edge—
batting & backing
trimmed even with
quilt top

Butterscotch Pudding

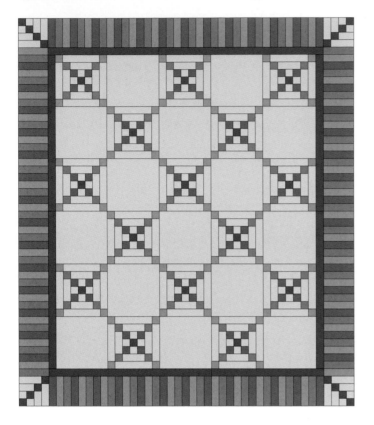

Photo on page 64. Method 1, page 6.

Approximate size 90x104″

14″ blocks set alternately with plain setting blocks

Use 42-45″-wide fabric. When strips appear in the cutting list, cut crossgrain strips (selvage to selvage).

Yardage

Background tan	6 yd
Border 1, center squares in chain blocks, & corner blocks purple	⅞ yd
Border 2 & squares in chain blocks red, blue, green	1½ yd each of 3 fabrics
Backing	8½ yd
Binding	⅞ yd
Batting – **thin** cotton or cotton blend	2 pieces 58x96″

Cutting

Pieced Blocks

tan	19 strips 2½″ wide
	2 strips 6½″ wide
	2 strips 10½″ wide
red, blue, green	4 strips 2½″ wide of ea. fabric
purple	1 strip 2½″ wide
Setting blocks tan	15 squares 14½″
Corner blocks tan	3 strips 2½″ wide
purple	16 squares 2½″
Border 1 purple	8 strips 2½″ wide
Border 2 red, blue, green	54 rectangles 2½x8½″ of each fabric
Binding	10 strips 2½″ wide

Directions

Use ¼″ seam allowance unless otherwise noted.

Please read General Directions, page 4.

1. Make Strip Sets A-D, as shown. Press. Crosscut into 2½″ segments. Crosscut remaining tan 2½″ strips into 30 segments 6½″ wide and 30 segments 10½″ wide.

2. Make 15 pieced blocks using segments from Step 1, as shown. Press.

3. For corner blocks, cut tan 2½″ strips into 8 squares 2½″, 8 rectangles 2½x4½″, and 8 rectangles 2½x6½″. Make 4 corner blocks as shown using tan pieces and purple squares. Press.

4. Lay blocks on floor, alternating with 14½″ setting blocks. Stitch blocks into horizontal rows as shown. Press.

5. Stitch top 3 rows together. Press. Stitch bottom 3 rows together. Press. See page 35.

6. Border 1 (diagrams on page 35)

    a. Measure length of top section of quilt. Cut border strips to the measured length and stitch to sides. Press. Repeat for bottom section of quilt.

    b. Measure width of top section of quilt. Piece strips to the measured length and stitch to top edge. Press. Repeat for bottom section of quilt, stitching border to bottom edge. Press.

7. Border 2: Lay quilt center sections on floor. Lay Border 2 rectangles around quilt, starting at top left of quilt and working clockwise. The three colors will rotate around the quilt evenly. Stitch 22 rectangles together for side borders of each section of quilt and sew to sides. Stitch 37 rectangles together for top and bottom borders. Sew corner blocks to each end of top and bottom borders, rotating as shown. Stitch top border to top of quilt and bottom border to bottom.

8. Piece backing to 96″ wide x 116″ long, in 3 horizontal panels. Press seams. Cut in half horizontally.

9. Layer each quilt section with backing and batting. Pin or spray baste. Quilt as desired, with one restriction: The bottom section may be quilted to the edge, but the top section must have 2-3″ left unquilted along bottom edge for joining. See diagrams on page 35.

   Note: Borders may be quilted now or after joining the two sections of the quilt. If quilting now, choose a design that will look okay across the space at the join, or do a meander pattern that can be filled in after the two sections of the quilt are joined.

10. Join the two sections, referring also to General Directions, Method 1, page 6. See diagrams on page 35.

a. Trim batting and backing **even with quilt top on top edge of bottom section of quilt only**.

b. On **bottom edge of top section** of quilt, trim batting and backing ½″ **from edge of quilt top** (½″ extends beyond quilt top).

c. Pin top and bottom sections of quilt together including all three layers of quilt on bottom section and only the quilt top on the top section. Pin well, easing in any fullness. Stitch.

d. Press seam allowance toward top section of quilt. Fold backing away from batting on top section of quilt and trim batting to just meet edge of batting on bottom section of quilt.

e. Hand whip edges together.

f. Turn under backing on top section of quilt to cover stitching line and hand stitch.

11. Finish any remaining quilting at join and in borders.

12. Trim remaining backing and batting even with quilt top.

13. Stitch binding strips end to end. Press in half lengthwise, wrong sides together. Bind quilt using ⅜″ seam allowance.

More diagrams on page 35.

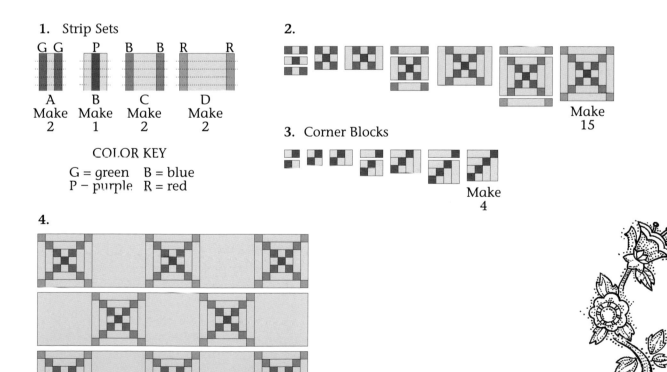

1. Strip Sets

G G   P   B B R   R

A   B   C   D
Make   Make   Make   Make
  2   1   2   2

COLOR KEY

G = green   B = blue
P – purple   R = red

2.

Make
15

3. Corner Blocks

Make
4

4.

37

Ice Crystals

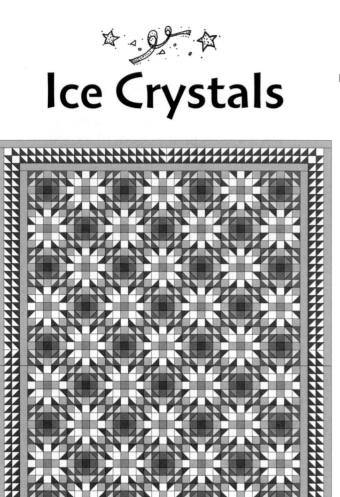

Photo on page 53. Method 1, page 6.

Approximate size 86 x 106″

10″ blocks set 7 x 9

Use 42-45″-wide fabric. When strips appear in the cutting list, cut crossgrain strips (selvage to selvage).

Yardage

Blue # 1 (darkest)	1⅞ yd
Blue # 2 (dark)	1 yd
Blue # 3 (darker medium)	⅝ yd
Blue # 4 (lighter medium)	1⅜ yd
Blue # 5 (light)	2⅛ yd
Fuchsia	1¼ yd
White	2¼ yd
Borders 1 & 3 (can be same as Blue # 3)	1⅝ yd
Border 2 dark (can be same as Blue # 1)	1⅜ yd
Border 2 light (can be same as Blue # 5)	1⅜ yd

Backing		8 yd
Binding		⅞ yd
Batting – **thin** cotton or cotton blend		1 piece 92 x 64″
		1 piece 92 x 54″

Cutting

Blue # 1	Block A	256 squares 2⅞″
Blue # 2	Block A	128 squares 2½″
	Block B	31 squares 2½″
Blue # 3	Block A	64 squares 2⅞″
Blue # 4	Block A	128 squares 2½″
	Block B	124 squares 2½″
Blue # 5	Block A	192 squares 2⅞″
	Block B	124 squares 2½″
Fuchsia	Block A	32 squares 2½″
	Block B	124 squares 2⅞″
White	Block B	248 squares 2½″
		124 squares 2⅞″
	Border 2 corners	8 squares 2½″
Borders 1 & 3		19 strips 2½″ wide
Border 2 dark		172 squares 2⅞″
Border 2 light		172 squares 2⅞″
Binding		10 strips 2½″ wide

Directions

Use ¼″ seam allowance unless otherwise noted.

Please read General Directions, page 4.

1. Cut all 2⅞″ squares in **half** diagonally. Make 32 Block A and 31 Block B, as shown.

2. Stitch blocks together into 9 rows of 7, alternating, as shown.

3. Stitch top 5 rows together. Press. Stitch bottom 4 rows together. Press.

4. Border 1

   a. Measure length of top section of quilt. Piece strips, if necessary, and cut to the measured length. Stitch to sides. Repeat for bottom section of quilt.

   b. Measure width of top section of quilt. Piece strips to the measured length and stitch to top edge. Press. Repeat for bottom section of quilt, stitching border to bottom edge. Press.

5. Border 2: Make units as shown on page 40 using Blue # 1 and Blue #5. Squares at ends of top and bottom borders are white. Stitch units into border sections as shown. Stitch to top and bottom sections of quilt, sides first.

6. Border 3: Repeat Step 4.

7. Piece backing to 92″ wide x 118″ long, in 3 horizontal panels. Press seams. Cut apart horizontally into 1 piece 92x64″ and 1 piece 92x54″.

8. Layer each quilt section with backing and batting. Pin or spray baste. Quilt as desired, with one restriction: The bottom section may be quilted to the edge, but the top section must have 2-3″ left unquilted along the bottom edge for joining.

9. Join the two sections, referring also to General Directions, Method 1, page 6. See diagrams on page 40.

   a. Trim batting and backing *even with quilt top on top edge of bottom section of quilt only*.

   b. On *bottom edge of top section* of quilt, trim batting and backing ½″ *from edge of quilt top* (½″ extends beyond quilt top).

   c. Pin top and bottom sections of quilt together including all three layers of quilt on bottom section and only the quilt top on the top section. Pin well, easing in any fullness. Stitch.

   d. Press seam allowance toward top section of quilt. Fold backing away from batting on top section of quilt and trim batting to just meet edge of batting on bottom section of quilt.

   e. Hand whip edges together.

   f. Turn under backing on top section of quilt to cover stitching line and hand stitch.

10. Finish any remaining quilting across the join.

11. Trim remaining backing and batting even with quilt top.

12. Stitch binding strips end to end. Press in half lengthwise, wrong sides together. Bind quilt using ⅜″ seam allowance.

More diagrams on page 40.

1. Block A – For one block

Make 12
Blues 1 & 5

Make 4
Blues 1 & 3

Make 4
Blues 2 & 4

Make 4

Fuchsia

Make 32

Block B – For one block

Make 8
Fuchsia & white

Make 4 Corners:
Use fuchsia & white units from above & add Blue # 4 & white squares

Make 4
Blue # 5 & white

Blue # 2

Make 31

2.

39

Ice Crystals

Continued from page 39.

5. Border 2

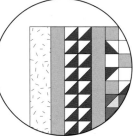 Make 344

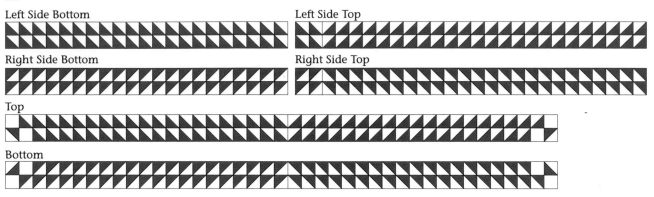

Left Side Bottom

Left Side Top

Right Side Bottom

Right Side Top

Top

Bottom

6.

Top Section

Bottom Section

9a. Bottom Section

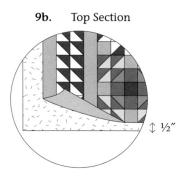

Quilted to edge—
batting & backing
trimmed even with
quilt top

9b. Top Section

1/2"

2-3" left unquilted—
batting & backing trimmed
1/2" from edge of quilt top

Indian Blanket

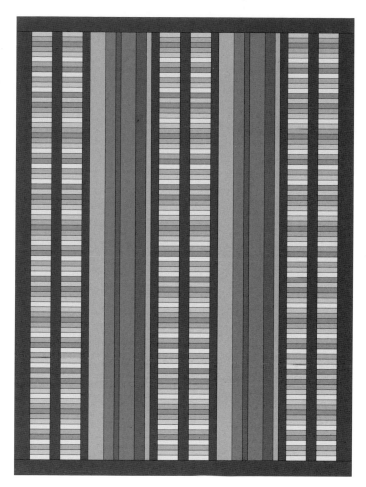

This quilt is reversible.
Photo on back cover.
Modified Method 2, page 7, & Method 4, page 9.

Approximate size 67x90″

Use 42-45″-wide fabric.

Yardage

Strata	golds, oranges blues, purples,	¼ yd each of 8 fabrics
	greens	¼ yd each of 8 fabrics
Vertical pieces	orange	*2⅝ yd (1¼ yd)
	gold	*2⅝ yd (1⅛ yd)
	blue	*2⅝ yd (⅞ yd)
Vertical pieces & seam-covering strips		
	navy	*2⅝ yd (2½ yd)
Border	navy	1⅛ yd (crosswise cuts)
Backing		8 yd
Binding		¾ yd
Batting – **thin** cotton		5 pieces 20x93″
or cotton blend		2 pieces 6x71″

*We recommend cutting these on the lengthwise grain for added stability, but have added yardage in parentheses for cutting on the crosswise grain.

Cutting

Strata	32 rectangles 1½x4½″ of each fabric
Verticals	see Step 2 below
Border	8 strips 3½″ wide (on crosswise grain)
Backing	5 pieces 20x93″ (on lengthwise grain)
	2 pieces 6x71″ (on lengthwise grain)
Binding	8 strips 2½″ wide (on crosswise grain)

Directions

Use ¼″ seam allowance unless otherwise noted.

Please read General Directions, page 4.

1. Stitch eighty-four 1½x4½″ gold/orange rectangles into 1 strata as shown on page 42. Make 2 more. Make 3 blue/purple/green strata. Press. Set aside.

2. Cut (or stitch strips together and then cut):

   Vertical Pieces:
   2 orange verticals 4½x84½″
   2 orange verticals 3x84½″
   2 gold verticals 2½x84½″
   2 gold verticals 3½x84½″
   2 blue verticals 1½x84½″
   2 blue verticals 2½x84½″
   3 navy verticals 2½x84½″

   Seam-covering strips—navy:
   8 pieces 3½x84½″

3. Layer backing piece wrong side up with batting piece. Basting spray works well. Make 5. Using permanent pen or water erasable marker, mark 3 batting pieces with 1 vertical line placed 9″ from left side and 2 horizontal lines 4″ from ends. Mark other 2 batting pieces with 1 vertical line placed 6″ from left side and 2 horizontal lines 4″ from ends. See diagram on page 42.

4. Make 3 strata sections as follows using batting pieces marked with vertical line 9″ from left. Place 1 gold/orange strata right side up along vertical line as shown. Place a navy vertical piece right side down on right edge of strata. Pin well. Stitch through all layers. Fold navy

Continued on page 42.

Indian Blanket

Continued from page 41.

piece over to right side and press lightly. Repeat with a blue/purple strata. See diagram. Make 2 more strata sections.

5. On 1 strata section, add 3½ x 84½" border piece to left side in same manner as other strips were added. Trim batting and backing even with border at right side. On second section, add border to right side and trim left side. On third section, trim both sides.

6. Make vertical sections: Lay 4½" orange vertical piece right side up along line. Pin 2½" gold vertical piece right side down on orange one. Stitch, fold over, press. Repeat with 1½" blue, 3½" gold, 2½" blue, and 3" orange vertical pieces. Make one more vertical section. Trim both sides of both vertical sections even with last vertical piece.

7. Lay all sections on floor and smooth edges. Pin edges of vertical sections well. Press seam-covering strips in half lengthwise, wrong sides together. Pin one seam-covering strip to right side and one to backing side of each strata edge, raw edges even. See diagram on page 43. Stitch through all layers. Refer also to General Directions, Method 2, page 7. Method 2 is modified in this quilt—the seam-covering strips are double thickness.

8. Join sections, referring also to General Directions, Method 2, page 7.

   a. Lay 2 left sections **edge to edge** and whip stitch to hold in place.

   b. Place under machine and zigzag together with widest stitch possible. Turn over and zigzag again from the back for extra hold.

   c. Fold over and lightly press seam-covering strip on back of quilt. On back, topstitch seam-covering strip to quilt ⅛" from fold. Note: This stitching should be covered by seam-covering strip on front of quilt. Test before continuing.

   d. On front, fold seam-covering strip to cover topstitching and hand stitch in place.

   e. Repeat Steps a-d for other 3 joins.

9. Add top and bottom borders, referring also to General Directions, Method 4, page 9.

   a. Layer and pin, raw edges even

      6 x 72" piece of batting
      6 x 72" piece of border backing, right side up
      top edge of quilt, right side up
      3½ x 68" Border 1 right side down, ends even with edges of side border pieces (trim to needed length)

   b. Stitch. Trim batting out of seam allowance as close to stitching line as possible. Fold Border 1, backing, and batting out away from quilt and press seam lightly on both front and back.

   c. Repeat at bottom edge of quilt.

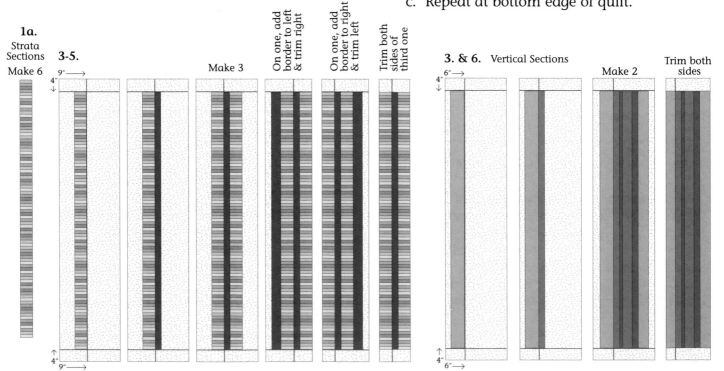

1a.
Strata Sections
Make 6

3-5.
9"→
4"↓

Make 3

On one, add border to left & trim right

On one, add border to right & trim left

Trim both sides of third one

4"
9"→

3. & 6. Vertical Sections
6"→
4"↓

Make 2

Trim both sides

4"
6"→

Dir

Use ¼'

Please

1. M
   Th
   a.

   b.

   c.

2. Mc
   fol
   ex
   Da

1.

2.

5.

Add

10.

Add

10. Trim remaining batting and backing even with quilt top.

11. Stitch binding strips end to end. Press in half lengthwise, wrong sides together. Bind quilt using ⅜" seam allowance.

7-8.

Pin and stitch seam-covering strips here

7-8b.

7-8b.

Backing

8c.

Machine Stitch

8d.

Hand Stitch

9a.

9b.

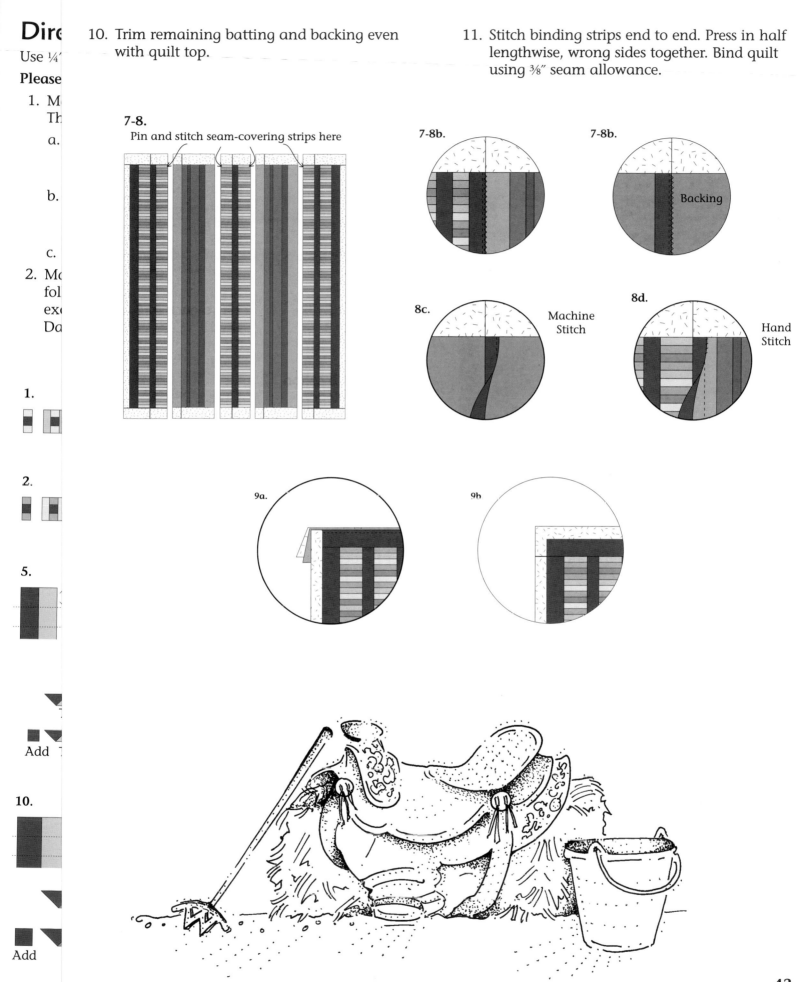

Mediterranean Tiles

Continued from page 45.

   d. Cut points off both sides of each strip, ¼" outside seam intersections. Borders should be 2½" wide. Trim ends as shown in diagram, ¼" outside seam intersection. Stitch 2½" corner squares to both ends of two of the borders.

   e. Stitch borders without corner squares to sides of applique center. Press. Stitch borders with corner squares to top and bottom. Press.

6. Inner Border 3: Cut or piece 2 Inner Border 3 strips 44½" long and stitch to sides. Cut or piece 2 Inner Border 3 strips 45½" long and stitch to top and bottom. Press. See diagram on page 47.

7. Inner row of Log Cabin blocks

   a. Stitch 5 inner row Log Cabin blocks together in a **vertical** row, lights at top and bottom and darks at sides. Make 2. Stitch to sides of quilt.

   b. Stitch 7 inner row Log Cabin blocks together in a **horizontal** row, lights at top and bottom and darks at sides. Make 2. Stitch to top and bottom of quilt.

8. Outer row of Log Cabin blocks

   a. Stitch 7 outer row Log Cabin blocks together in a **vertical** row, lights at sides and darks at top and bottom. Make 2. Stitch to sides of quilt.

   b. Stitch 9 outer row Log Cabin blocks together in a **horizontal** row, lights at sides and darks at top and bottom. Make 2. Stitch to top and bottom of quilt.

9. Outer Border 1: Piece 2 Outer Border 1 strips 81½" long and stitch to sides. Ease quilt to fit border, if necessary. Piece 2 Outer Border 1 strips 84½" long and stitch to top and bottom, again easing quilt to fit border. Press.

10. Outer Border 2

   a. Stitch 1 strip of each color into strip set as shown in diagram on page 45. Make 8 strip sets. Press seam allowances to the darkest fabric.

   b. Crosscut strip sets into 4¾" segments.

   c. Stitch 15 segments together as shown, offsetting each one by placing raw edge ¼" from seamline of previous segment

(**seamlines** of each segment match). Press seam allowances to the darkest fabric. Make 4.

   d. Cut points off both sides of each strip, ¼" outside seam intersections. Borders should be 3½" wide. Trim ends as shown in diagram, ¼" outside seam intersection. Stitch 3½" corner squares to both ends of 2 of the borders.

   e. Stitch borders without corner squares to sides of quilt. Press. Stitch borders with corner squares to top and bottom. Press.

11. Outer Border 3: Piece 2 Outer Border 3 strips 90½" long and stitch to sides. Piece 2 Outer Border 3 strips 92½" long and stitch to top and bottom. Press.

12. Piece backing to same size as batting. Layer backing, batting, and quilt top, but pin or spray baste **only the center** of the quilt, top edge to bottom edge, even with the applique portion of the quilt. Fold right side of quilt top and backing away from batting. Carefully cut batting away in a curvy line 3-4" wide. See General Directions, Method 3, page 8. Attach a label at the top front of the batting piece saying "top right". Set aside. Repeat for left side of quilt.

13. Quilt center section of quilt.

14. Lay quilt on floor, lift right side of quilt top, and replace batting, matching curves. Hand whip batting pieces together. Fold quilt top back in position. Pin or spray baste and quilt right side of quilt.

15. Repeat Step 14 for left side of quilt.

16. Trim remaining backing and batting even with quilt top.

17. Stitch binding strips end to end. Press in half lengthwise, wrong sides together. Bind quilt using ⅜" seam allowance.

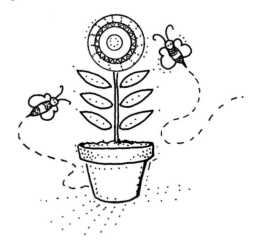

Phot
App
Use
cutti
Note
piec
sizes

Ya

Appl
Appl

Inne
Inne
Log (
  cer
  ligh
  ligh
  ligh
  dai
  dai
  dai

4.

5e.

6.

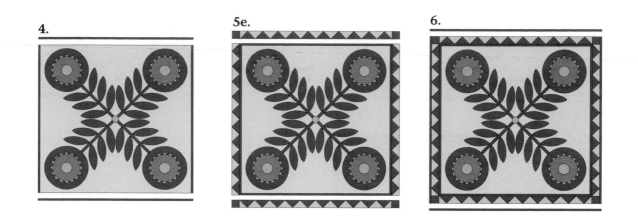

7.

8.

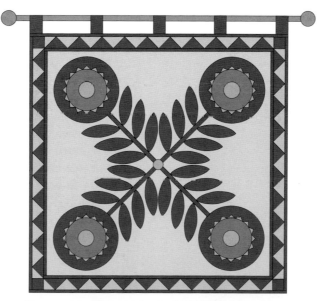

Try a smaller project: 45″ Wall Hanging

Dutch Treat

Photo on page 49. Method 1, page 6.

Approximate size 87x87″   9″ blocks set 9x9

Use 42-45″-wide fabric. When strips appear in the cutting list, cut crossgrain strips (selvage to selvage).

Note: Since this quilt is made up of multiple pieced borders, precise piecing is critical. Actual sizes of all pieces are given.

Yardage

Lone Star	dark blue	½ yd
	med blue	¾ yd
	light blue	⅓ yd
	yellow	¾ yd
Lone Star Border 1		
	dk blue	¼ yd
Lge setting triangles		1⅜ yd
Lone Star Border 2		
	yellow	⅓ yd
Log Cabins - sides		
centers - yellow		⅙ yd
row 1 - light blue		¼ yd
row 2 - light blue		⅜ yd
row 3 - med blue		⅜ yd
row 4 - med blue		⅝ yd
row 5 - dark blue		⅝ yd
row 6 - dark blue		¾ yd

Log Cabins – corners		Lone Star leftovers see cutting chart below
Nine-patches – sides		
light blue		1½ yd
med blue		½ yd
yellow		½ yd each of 4
Nine-patches - corners		
dark blue, med blue		¼ yd each
yellow		⅜ yd
Outer Border		1⅛ yd
Backing		8¼ yd
Binding		¾ yd
Batting – **thin** cotton or cotton blend		1 piece 51x93″ 2 pieces 27x93″

Cutting

Lone Star	dark blue	2 strips 3½″ wide
	med blue	4 strips 3½″ wide
	light blue	2 strips 3½″ wide
	yellow	4 squares 9″
	yellow	1 square 13¼″
Lone Star Border 1		4 strips 1½″ wide
Setting triangles		2 squares 22⅜″
Lone Star Border 2		5 strips 1½″ wide

Log Cabins - 20 blocks for sides

centers	20 squares 2″
row 1	40 rectangles 1¾x2″
row 2	40 rectangles 1¾x4½″
row 3	40 rectangles 1¾x4½″
row 4	40 rectangles 1¾x7″
row 5	40 rectangles 1¾x7″
row 6	40 rectangles 1¾x9½″

Log Cabins - 4 blocks for corners - use Lone Star leftovers

centers - med blue	4 squares 2″
row 1 - yellow	8 rectangles 1¾x2″
row 2 - yellow	8 rectangles 1¾x4½″
row 3 - med blue	8 rectangles 1¾x4½″
row 4 - med blue	8 rectangles 1¾x7″
row 5 - dk blue	8 rectangles 1¾x7″
row 6 - dk blue	8 rectangles 1¾x9½″

Nine-patches - 28 blocks for sides

light blue	12 strips 3½″ wide
med blue	3 strips 3½″ wide
yellow	3 strips 3½″ wide of each fabric

Continued on page 50.

Ice Crystals, page 38   **53**

Pinecones & Berries

Photo on page 57. Method 1, page 6.

Approximate size 95x107″

12″ blocks set 7x8

Use 42-45″-wide fabric. When strips appear in the cutting list, cut crossgrain strips (selvage to selvage).

Yardage

Light – tan	2⅜ yd
Medium – rust print	2¼ yd
Medium – large print	2 yd
Dark – green	3⅛ yd
Border 1	¾ yd
Border 2	1⅝ yd
Backing	8¾ yd
Binding	⅞ yd
Batting – **thin** cotton or cotton blend	2 pieces 101x59″

Cutting

Block A – tan	56 squares 4⅞″
Block A – rust print	84 squares 4½″
	28 squares 4⅞″
Block A – green	84 squares 4⅞″
Block B – tan	112 squares 3½″
Block B – large print	28 squares 9″
Block B – green	112 squares 3⅞″
Border 1	10 strips 2″ wide
Border 2	11 strips 4½″ wide
Binding	11 strips 2½″ wide

Directions

Use ¼″ seam allowance unless otherwise noted.

Please read General Directions, page 4.

1. Cut 3⅞″ and 4⅞″ squares in **half** diagonally. Make 28 Block A and 28 Block B as shown. Press.

2. Stitch blocks together into 8 rows of 7, rotating Block A in alternate rows, as shown.

3. Stitch top 4 rows together. Press. Stitch bottom 4 rows together. Press.

4. Border 1

   a. Measure length of top section of quilt. Piece strips to the measured length and stitch to sides. Repeat for bottom section of quilt.

   b. Measure width of top section of quilt. Piece strips to the measured length and stitch to top edge. Repeat for bottom section of quilt, stitching border to bottom edge. Press.

5. Border 2: Repeat Step 4.

6. Piece backing to 101″ wide x 118″ long, in 3 horizontal panels. Press seams. Cut apart horizontally into 2 pieces 101x59″.

7. Layer each quilt section with backing and batting. Pin or spray baste. Quilt as desired, with one restriction: The bottom section may be quilted to the edge, but the top section must have 2-3″ left unquilted along the bottom edge for joining.

   Note: Borders can be quilted now or after joining the two sections of the quilt. If quilting now, choose a design that will look okay across the space at the join, or do a meander pattern that can be filled in after the two sections of the quilt are joined.

54

8. Join the two sections, referring also to General Directions, Method 1, page 6.

   a. Trim batting and backing **even with quilt top on top edge of bottom section of quilt only**.

   b. On **bottom edge of top section** of quilt, trim batting and backing ½″ **from edge of quilt top** (½″ extends beyond quilt top).

   c. Pin top and bottom sections of quilt together including all three layers of quilt on bottom section and only the quilt top on the top section. Pin well, easing in any fullness. Stitch.

   d. Press seam allowance toward top section of quilt. Fold backing away from batting on top section of quilt and trim batting to just meet edge of batting on bottom section of quilt.

   e. Hand whip edges together.

   f. Turn under backing on top section of quilt to cover stitching line and hand stitch.

9. Finish any remaining quilting at the join and in borders.

10. Trim remaining backing and batting even with quilt top.

11. Stitch binding strips end to end. Press in half lengthwise, wrong sides together. Bind quilt using ⅜″ seam allowance.

1. For one Block A

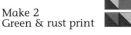
Make 4
Green & tan

Make 2
Green & rust print

For one Block B

Make 4
Green & tan

7-8a. Bottom Section

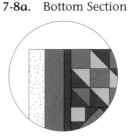

Quilted to edge—
batting & backing
trimmed even with
quilt top

2-3. Make 2, one top section & one bottom section

4-5. Top Section

Bottom Section

7-8b. Top Section

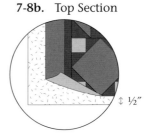

↕ ½″

2-3″ left unquilted—
batting & backing trimmed
½″ from edge of quilt top

55

Vanilla Ice Cream

This quilt is reversible.

Photo on page 29. Method 2, page 7.

Approximate size 67x90"

16" blocks set diagonally

Use 42-45"-wide fabric. When strips appear in the cutting list, cut crossgrain strips (selvage to selvage).

Yardage

Top of quilt incl. blocks, side triangles,
& seam-covering strips

	7½ yd cream
Backing # 1	
Blocks	⅝ yd each of 9-18 fabrics
Backing # 2	
Side triangles	2¼ yd contrasting fabric
Backing # 3	
Seam-covering strips	1 yd
Binding	¾ yd

Batting – **thin** cotton
or cotton blend   23 squares 18"
                          2 squares 13"

Cutting

Cream

center blocks & side triangles	23 squares 18"
corner triangles	2 squares 13"
seam-covering strips	20-24 strips 1¼" wide
Backing(s) # 1	18 squares 18"
Backing # 2	5 squares 18"
	2 squares 13"
Backing # 3	20-24 strips 1¼" wide
Binding	8 strips 2½" wide

Directions

Use ¼" seam allowance unless otherwise noted.

Please read General Directions, page 4.

1. Make 12 quilted motif blocks (18"). Layer backing # 1, batting, and cream squares. Quilt with desired quilting patterns designed for 16" blocks, centering designs. Diagram at left shows blocks quilted with adaptations of applique patterns from Indigo Braids quilt, pages 73-74. Trim blocks to 16" square.

2. Make 6 blocks (18") with backing # 1, batting, and cream squares. Crosshatch quilt 2" apart. Trim blocks to 16" square.

3. Make 5 blocks (18") with backing # 2, batting, and cream squares. Channel quilt 2" apart as shown. Trim blocks to 16" square. Cut in half diagonally as shown.

4. Make 2 blocks (13") with backing # 2, batting, and cream squares. Channel quilt 2" apart as shown. Trim blocks to 11⅜" square. Cut in half diagonally as shown.

5. Lay blocks on floor, placing them with the various backings in desired positions. Join blocks into diagonal rows, referring also to General Directions, Method 2, page 7.

   a. Work with one join at a time. Pin 1¼" seam-covering strips to both sides of one edge of a quilted square, right sides together, raw edges even. (Cream strip should be right side down on the top of the square, and Backing # 3 strip should be right side against the quilt backing, all raw edges even.) Stitch through all layers with ¼" seam allowance.

b. Lay square with seam-covering strips **edge to edge** with a square without strips and stitch together with widest zigzag possible. Turn over and zigzag from other side. Continue joining blocks in each row in this way.

c. On back of each row of blocks, turn under raw edge of each seam-covering strip to meet stitching line. Press. Fold strip over to cover seam. Topstitch close to fold.

d. On front of each row, turn under just enough seam allowance of each seam-covering strip to cover topstitching from Step c and hand stitch in place.

6. Stitch enough seam-covering strips together end to end for each set of rows to be joined. Join rows together using method in Step 5, making sure seam-covering strips line up from row to row.

7. Stitch binding strips end to end. Press in half lengthwise, wrong sides together. Bind quilt using ⅜" seam allowance.

3.   **4.**

5.

5a.

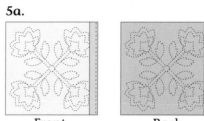

Front   Back

5b. Front   Front

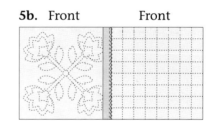

5b.

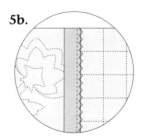

6.

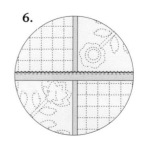

Susie's Flowerpots

Photo on page 60. Method 4, page 9.

Approximate size 66x88"

Use 42-45"-wide fabric. When strips appear in the cutting list, cut crossgrain strips (selvage to selvage).

Yardage

Applique backgrnd	2 yd
2nd color (bottom)	¼ yd
Corner blocks	⅜ yd
2nd color (bottom)	¼ yd
Appliques	⅛ yd each of 5 greens (leaves)
	bright scraps to total 1½ yd (flowers, birds, bees)
	¾ yd green (vine)
	¼ yd (pots)
	⅛ yd each of 2-3 fabrics (top rims of pots and & grass in pots)
Border 1	½ yd
Border 2 & sashing	2¾ yd
Sashing 2nd color	¾ yd

Backing – Quilt Center	3¼ yd
Backing – Border 2	2½ yd (must have 44" usable width) (consider using fabric that contrasts with backing for center of quilt)
Binding	¾ yd
Batting – **thin** cotton or cotton blend	1 piece 54x76" (center)
	2 pieces 11x70" (top/bottom)
	2 pieces 11x76" (sides)

Cutting Patterns on pages 69-72

Note: Our favorite method of applique is fusible web, and our patterns are set up for it—reversed for tracing and no seam allowances added.

Applique background	3 pieces 10½x64" cut on lengthwise grain
Appl. bkg. (bottom)	3 rectangles 10½x5"
Appliques	see pages 69-72
Vine	1¼"-wide **bias** strips totaling 240" in length
Sashing (Border 2 fabric)	7-8 strips 2½" wide
Sashing (2nd color)	7-8 strips 2½" wide
Border 1	6-7 strips 1½" wide
Border 2	2 strips 9½x48½" cut on lengthwise grain
	2 strips 9½x70½" cut on lengthwise grain
Corner blocks	4 squares 9½x9½"
Corner block (bottom)	1 strip 5" wide
Backing – Quilt Center	2 pieces 55" x fabric width
Backing – Border 2	2 pieces 11x76" cut on lengthwise grain
	2 pieces 11x70" cut on lengthwise grain
Binding	8 strips 2½" wide

Directions

Use ¼" seam allowance unless otherwise noted.

Please read General Directions, page 4.

1. Stitch bottom applique background rectangles to applique backgrounds. Stitch sashing strips into four 68½" lengths of each color. Stitch one sashing strip to each side of each background as shown. Press.

2. Applique

   a. Trace appliques to fusible web.

b. Fuse to desired fabrics and cut out.

c. Stitch bias strips end to end to make 240″ long. Press in thirds lengthwise, to wrong side, creating a bias strip with 2 folds that is approximately ½″ wide.

d. On each background strip, arrange pot and vine, using photo and diagrams as guides for placement. If desired, lay flowers on vine temporarily, to aid in placement of vine. Pin or glue baste vine in position. Topstitch along both edges of vine, turning under raw ends as needed.

e. Arrange flowers, leaves, birds, and bees along vine. Fuse. Stitch in place with machine zigzag or buttonhole stitch.

f. Corner Blocks: Fuse 5″ strip of corner block bottom fabric. Cut four 3x9½″ rectangles from fused fabric. Curvy cut the top edges to look like the ones in the diagrams. Place one on bottom of each corner block and arrange bird appliques. Fuse. Stitch in place as in Step 2e.

3. Stitch applique rows and remaining sashing rows together. See diagram. Press.

4. Border 1: Stitch strips into two 48½″ lengths and two 68½″ lengths. Stitch 68½″ pieces to sides. Stitch 48½″ pieces to top and bottom. Press.

5. Piece backing for quilt center horizontally to 54x76″. Layer quilt center with backing and batting. Pin or spray baste and quilt. Quilting can be done as close to edge as desired. Trim batting and backing even with quilt top on all sides.

6. Border 2: Refer also to General Directions, Method 4, page 9. See diagrams on page 65.

   a. Layer and pin, raw edges even:

      11x76″ piece of batting
      11x76″ border backing, right side up
      Right edge of quilt, right side up
      9½x70½″ Border 2, right side down

   b. Stitch. Trim batting out of seam allowance as close to stitching line as possible. Fold Border 2, backing, and batting out away from quilt and press seam lightly on both front and back.

Continued on page 65.

1.

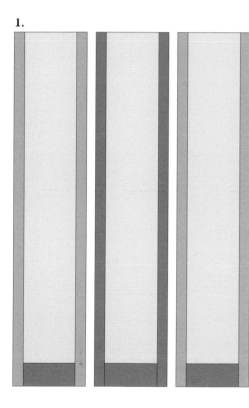

2d.

3.

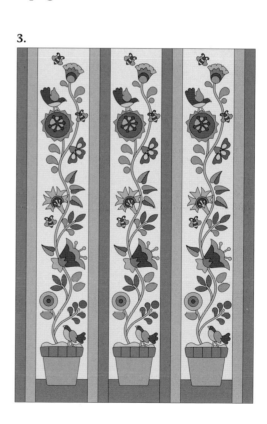

2f.

Butterscotch Pudding, page 36

Susie's Flowerpots

Continued from page 63.

c. Repeat Steps a and b at left edge of quilt.

d. Trim backing and batting even with quilt at top and bottom.

e. Stitch corner blocks to each end of each 9½ x 48½" Border 2 piece, birds facing inward.

f. Layer and pin, raw edges even, easing in any fullness:

    11 x 70" piece of batting
    11 x 70" border backing, right side up
    Top edge of quilt, right side up
    Border 2 with corner blocks attached,
        right side down

g. Repeat Step b.

h. Repeat Steps f-g at bottom edge of quilt.

7. Quilt borders.

8. Trim remaining batting and backing even with quilt top.

9. Stitch binding strips end to end. Press in half lengthwise, wrong sides together. Bind quilt using ⅜" seam allowance.

6d.

Trim

Trim

6e.

6f-g.

Decorate a shower curtain with the patterns from Susie's Flowerpots

Salsa

Photo on page 61. Method 1, page 6.

Approximate size 66x86″

10″ blocks set 5x7

Use 42-45″-wide fabric. When strips appear in the cutting list, cut crossgrain strips (selvage to selvage).

Yardage

Yellow	½ yd
Gold	1⅜ yd
Orange	1 yd
Rust	1⅓ yd
Purple # 1 (dark solid)	¼ yd
Purple # 2 (light solid)	⅞ yd
Purple (dot)	⅞ yd
Purple (stripe)	⅜ yd
Green	½ yd
Border 1 (light purple)	⅓ yd
Border 2 (orange)	½ yd
Border 3 (purple dot & gold)	1⅛ yd each of 2 fabrics
Border 4 (dark purple)	¾ yd
Backing	5¾ yd
Binding	¾ yd
Batting – **thin** cotton or cotton blend	1 piece 72x44″
	1 piece 72x54″

Cutting

Yellow	Block B	68 squares 2½″
Gold	Block B	136 squares 2½″
	Block B	68 squares 2⅞″
Orange	Block A	108 squares 2⅞″
Rust	Block A	108 squares 2⅞″
	Block A	72 squares 2½″
Purple # 1	Block A	18 squares 2½″
Purple # 2	Block A	72 squares 2½″
	Block A	36 squares 2⅞″
Purple stripe	Block A	36 squares 2⅞″
Purple dot	Block B	17 squares 2½″
	Block B	68 squares 2⅞″
Green	Block B	68 squares 2½″
Border 1		6-7 strips 1¼″ wide
Border 2		7 strips 1¾″ wide
Border 3 dark		136 squares 2⅞″
Border 3 light		136 squares 2⅞″
Border 4		8 strips 2½″ wide
Binding		8 strips 2½″ wide

Directions

Use ¼″ seam allowance unless otherwise noted.

Please read General Directions, page 4.

1. Cut all 2⅞″ squares in **half** diagonally. Make 18 Block A and 17 Block B, as shown.

2. Stitch blocks together into 7 rows of 5, alternating, as shown.

3. Stitch top 4 rows together. Press. Stitch bottom 3 rows together. Press.

4. Border 1

   a. Measure length of top section of quilt. Piece strips, if necessary, and cut to the measured length. Stitch to sides. Repeat for bottom section of quilt.

   b. Measure width of top section of quilt. Piece strips to the measured length and stitch to top edge. Press. Repeat for bottom section of quilt, stitching border to bottom edge. Press.

5. Border 2: Repeat Step 4.

6. Border 3: Make 272 units as shown in diagram on page 68. Stitch units into border sections as shown. Stitch to top and bottom sections of quilt, sides first.

7. Border 4: Repeat Step 4.

8. Piece backing to 72″ wide x 98″ long, in 2 vertical panels. Press seam. Cut apart horizontally into 1 piece 72x44″ and 1 piece 72x54″.

9. Layer each quilt section with backing and batting. Pin or spray baste. Quilt as desired, with one restriction: The bottom section may be quilted to the edge, but the top section must have 2-3″ left unquilted along the bottom edge for joining.

10. Join the two sections, referring also to General Directions, Method 1, page 6. See page 68 for diagrams.

    a. Trim batting and backing *even with quilt top on top edge of bottom section of quilt only*.

    b. On *bottom edge of top section* of quilt, trim batting and backing ½″ *from edge of quilt top* (½″ extends beyond quilt top).

    c. Pin top and bottom sections of quilt together including all three layers of quilt on bottom section and only the quilt top on the top section. Pin well, easing in any fullness. Stitch.

    d. Press seam allowance toward top section of quilt. Fold backing away from batting on top section of quilt and trim batting to just meet edge of batting on bottom section of quilt.

    e. Hand whip edges together.

    f. Turn under backing on top section of quilt to cover stitching line and hand stitch.

11. Finish any remaining quilting at join.

12. Trim remaining backing and batting even with quilt top.

13. Stitch binding strips end to end. Press in half lengthwise, wrong sides together. Bind quilt using ⅜″ seam allowance.

More diagrams on page 68.

1. Block A – For one block

Make 12
Rust & orange

Make 4
Purple # 2
& purple stripe

Make 4
Purple # 2
& rust

Make 4

Make 18

Purple # 1

Block B – For one block

Make 8
Gold &
purple dot

Make 4
Gold &
yellow

Make 4 corners:
Use gold & purple dot units
from above and add green
& gold squares

Make 17

Purple dot

2.

Salsa

Continued from page 67.

6. Border 3

 Make 272

Left Side of Bottom Section

Left Side of Top Section

Right Side of Bottom Section

Right Side of Top Section

Top

Bottom

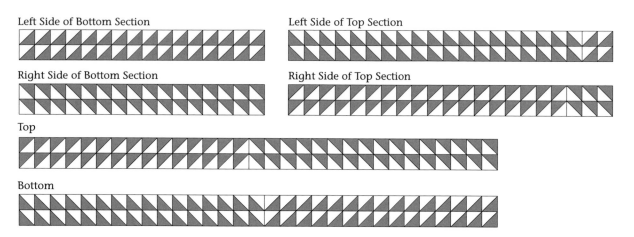

7.

Top Section

Bottom Section

10a.
Bottom Section

Quilted to edge—
batting & backing
trimmed even with
quilt top

10b.
Top Section

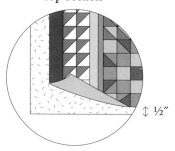

⬍ ½"

2-3" left unquilted—
batting & backing trimmed
½" from edge of quilt top

68

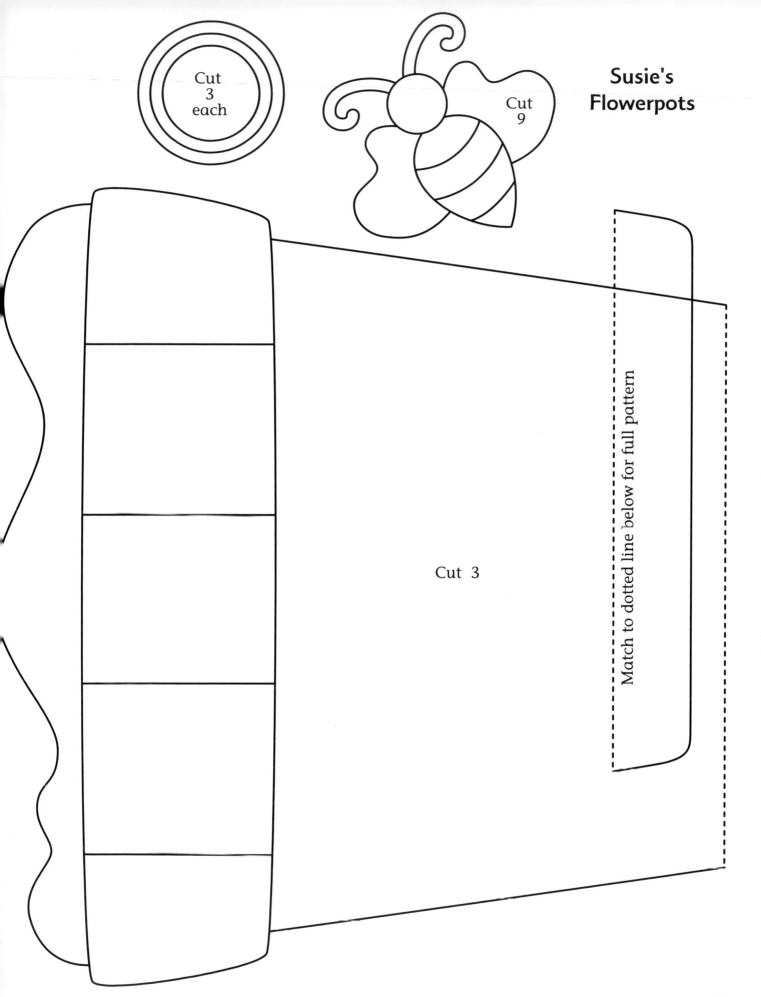

Cut
3
each

Cut
9

Susie's
Flowerpots

Cut 3

Match to dotted line below for full pattern

69

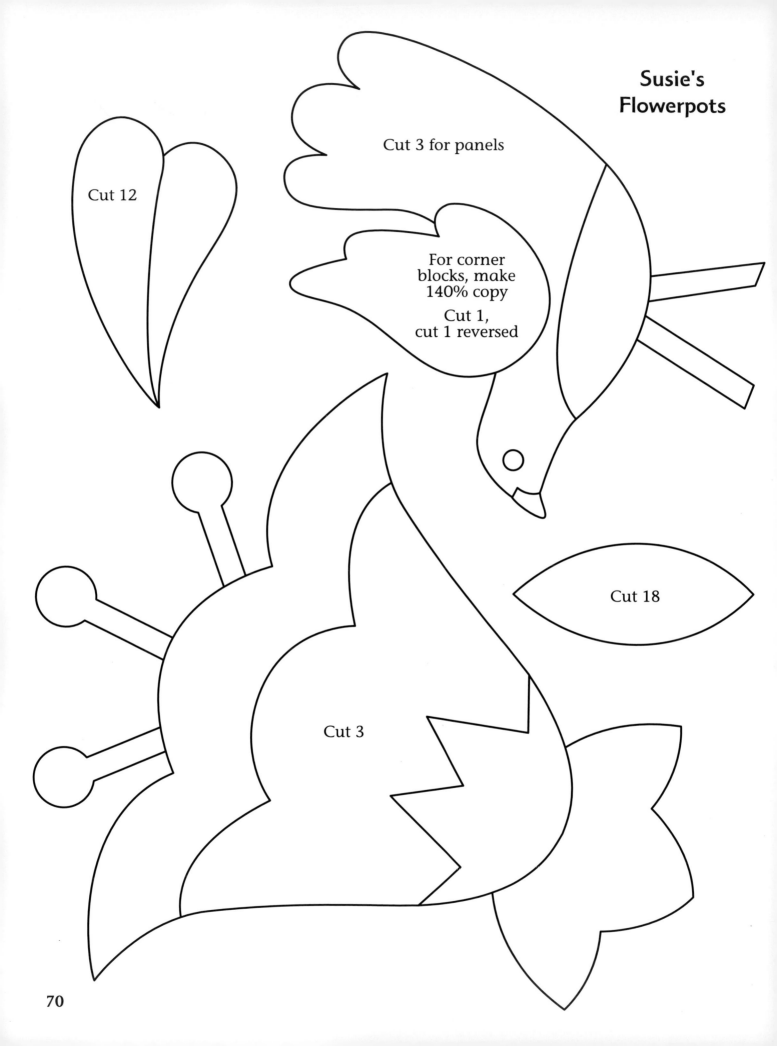

Susie's
Flowerpots

Cut 12

Cut 3 for panels

For corner
blocks, make
140% copy

Cut 1,
cut 1 reversed

Cut 18

Cut 3

70

Susie's Flowerpots

Cut 6
Cut 3 reversed

Cut 3

Cut 12

Cut 9
reversed

Cut 9

Cut 3

Cut 3

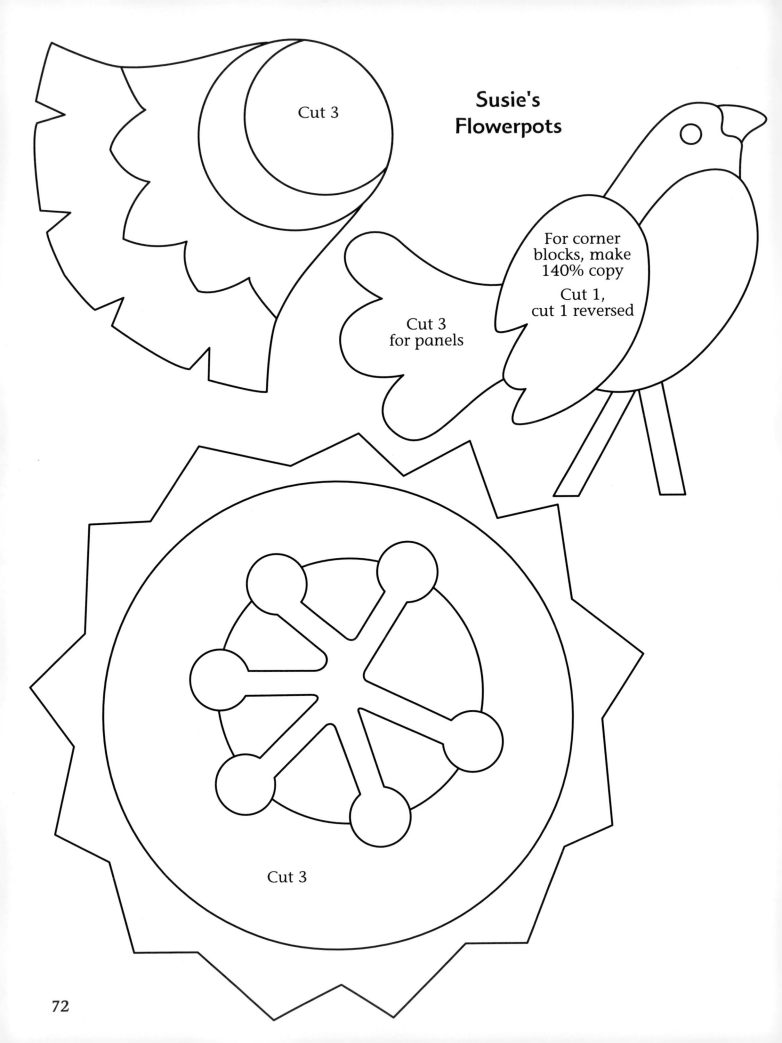

Cut 3

Susie's Flowerpots

For corner blocks, make 140% copy

Cut 1, cut 1 reversed

Cut 3 for panels

Cut 3

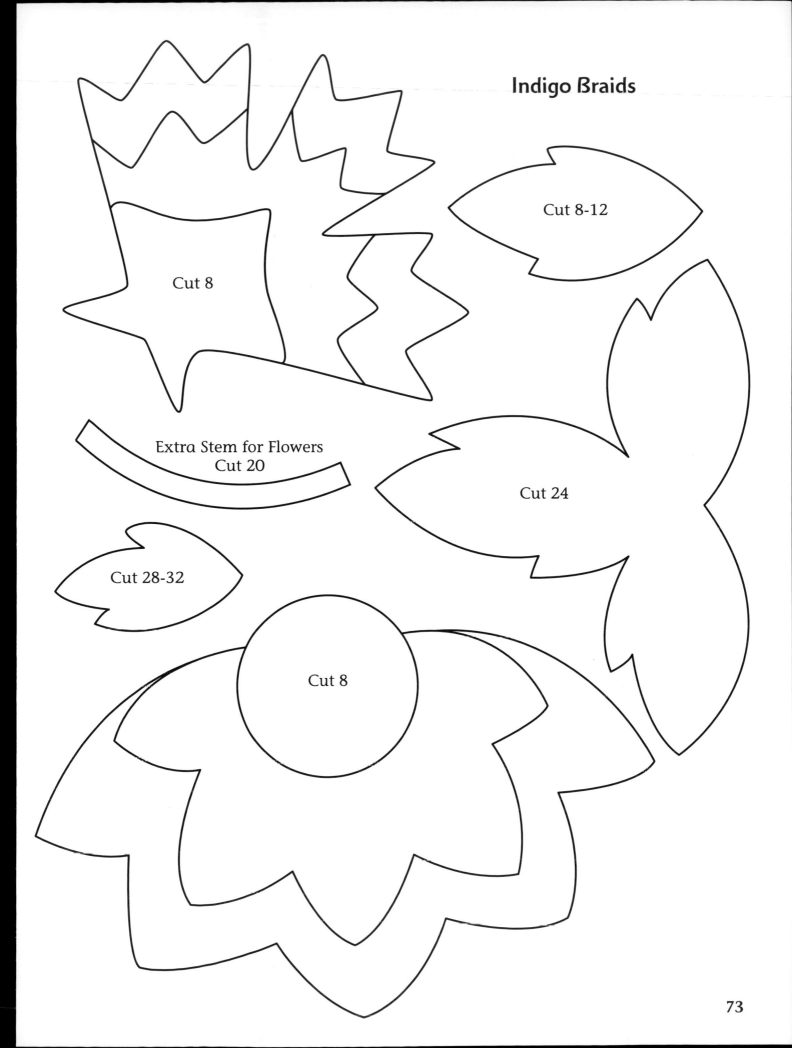

Cut 8-12

Cut 8

Cut 24

Extra Stem for Flowers
Cut 20

Cut 28-32

Cut 8

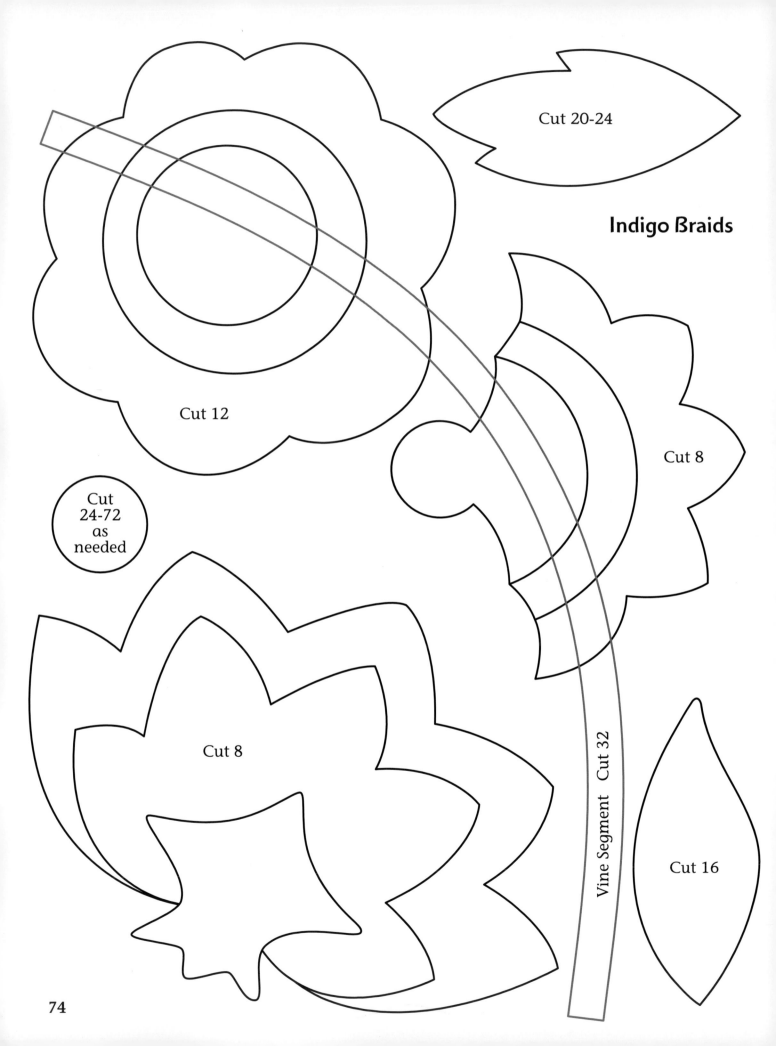

Cut 20-24

Indigo Braids

Cut 12

Cut
24-72
as
needed

Cut 8

Cut 8

Vine Segment Cut 32

Cut 16

Midnight Garden

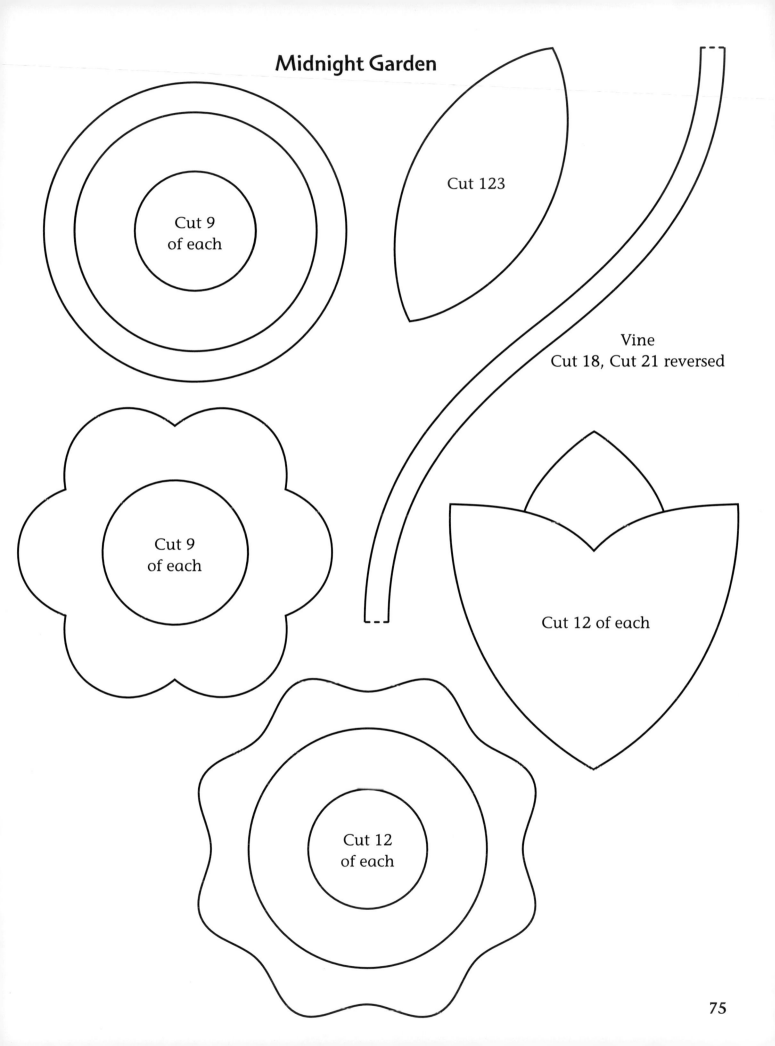

Cut 9
of each

Cut 123

Vine
Cut 18, Cut 21 reversed

Cut 9
of each

Cut 12 of each

Cut 12
of each

75

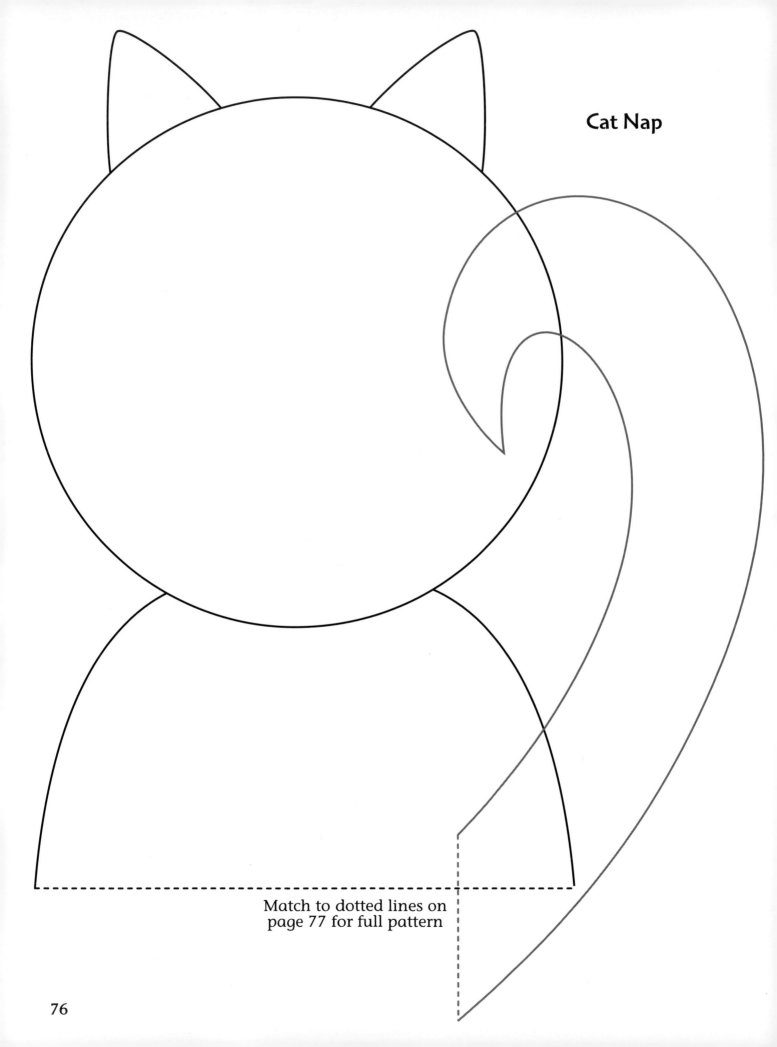

Cat Nap

Match to dotted lines on
page 77 for full pattern

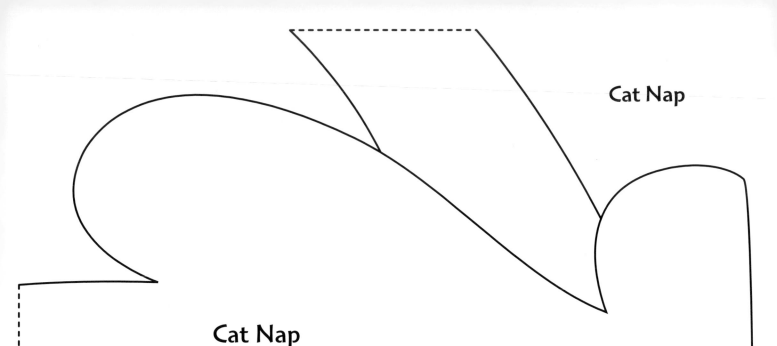

Cat Nap

Continued from page 23.

    b. On top edge of quilt, pin Border 2, right sides together, raw edges even, to Border 1 through backing and batting. Make sure strip cut from Border 1 fabric lines up with Border 1 on sides of quilt. Stitch through all layers. Fold border over and press lightly.

    c. Repeat at bottom of quilt.

    d. If desired, quilt in seams on both sides of 1″-wide rectangles.

8. Trim batting and backing even with quilt top.

9. Stitch binding strips end to end. Press in half lengthwise, wrong sides together. Bind quilt using ⅜″ seam allowance.

10. Applique cat and feathers to quilt using whole-quilt diagram and photo as guides. Machine stitching will show on back of quilt.

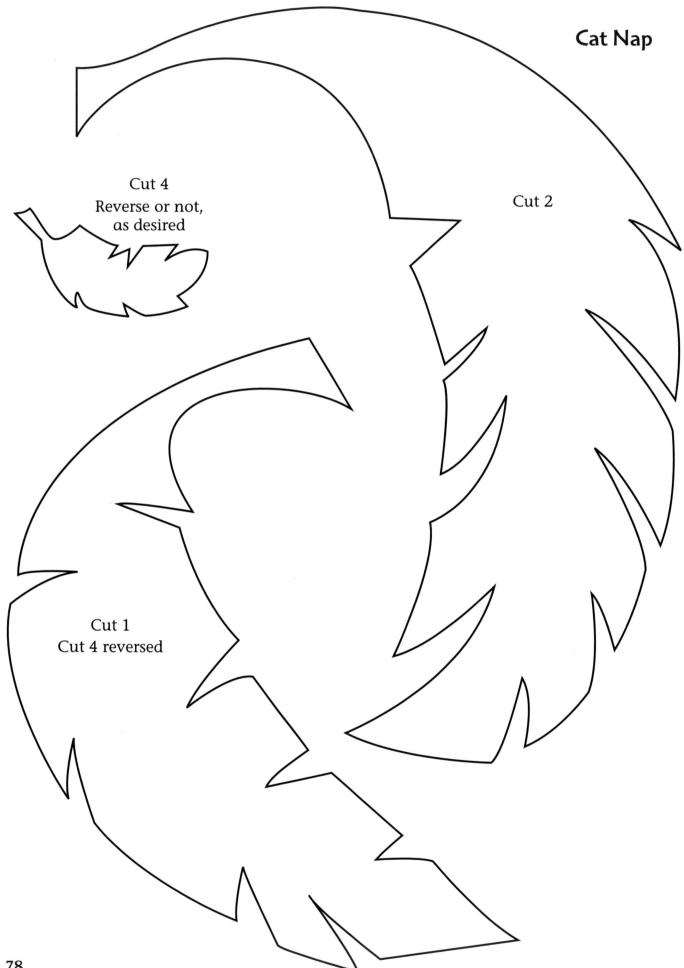

Cat Nap

Cut 4
Reverse or not,
as desired

Cut 2

Cut 1
Cut 4 reversed

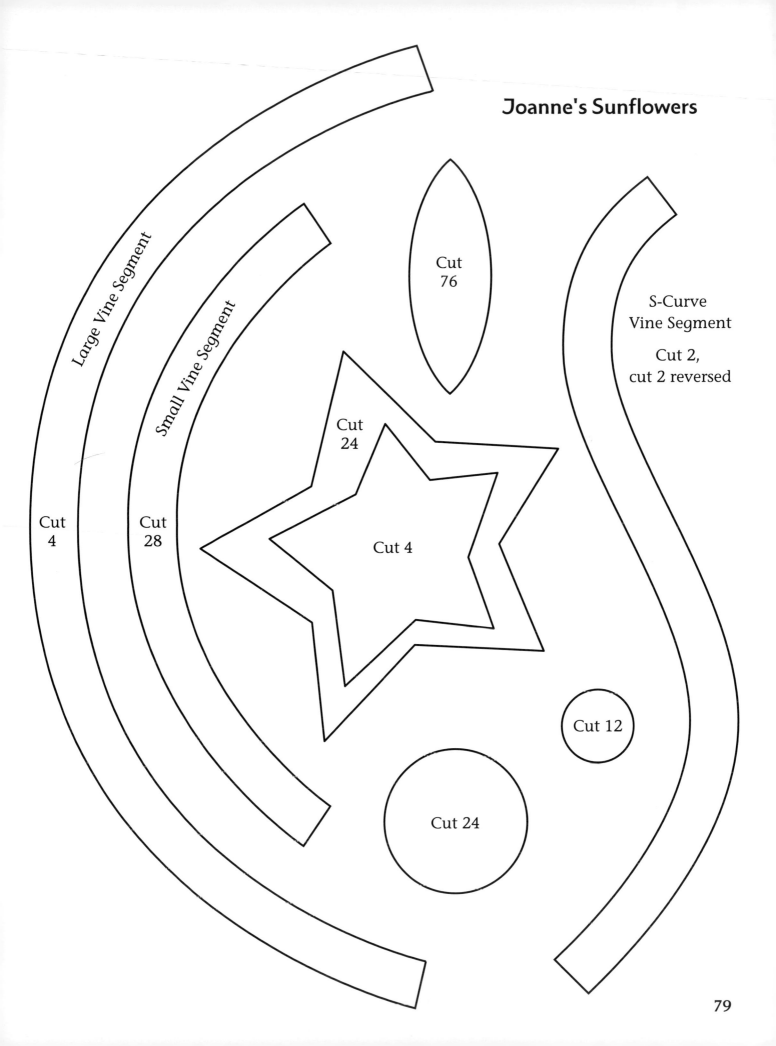

Joanne's Sunflowers

Large Vine Segment

Cut
4

Small Vine Segment

Cut
28

Cut
76

S-Curve
Vine Segment

Cut 2,
cut 2 reversed

Cut
24

Cut 4

Cut 12

Cut 24

79

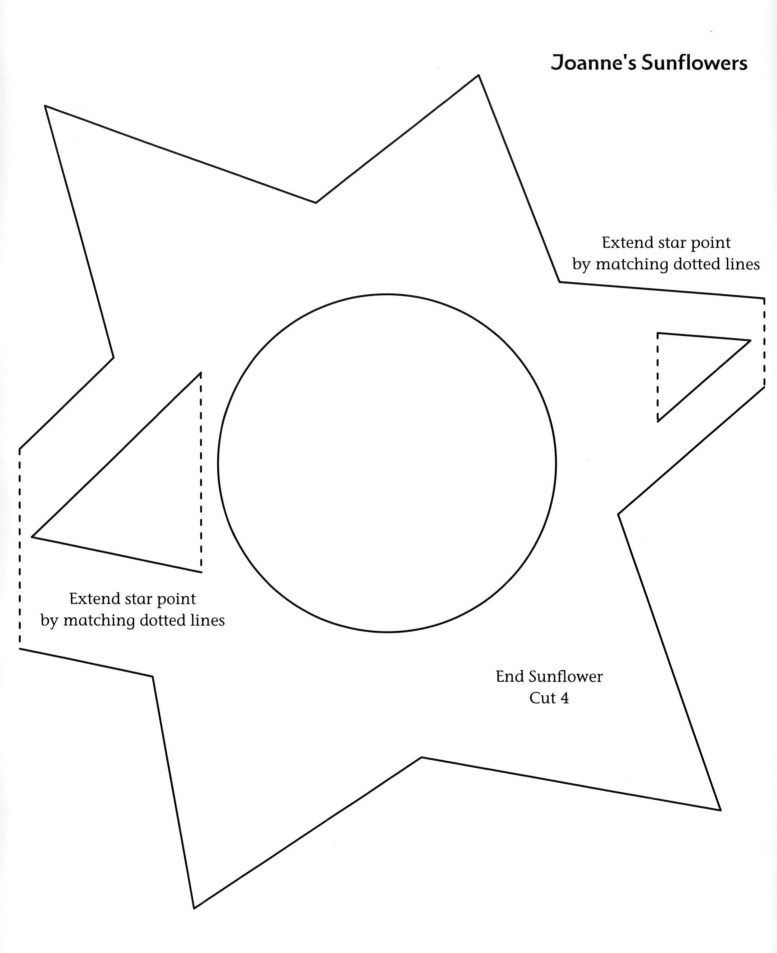

Joanne's Sunflowers

Extend star point
by matching dotted lines

Extend star point
by matching dotted lines

End Sunflower
Cut 4

80

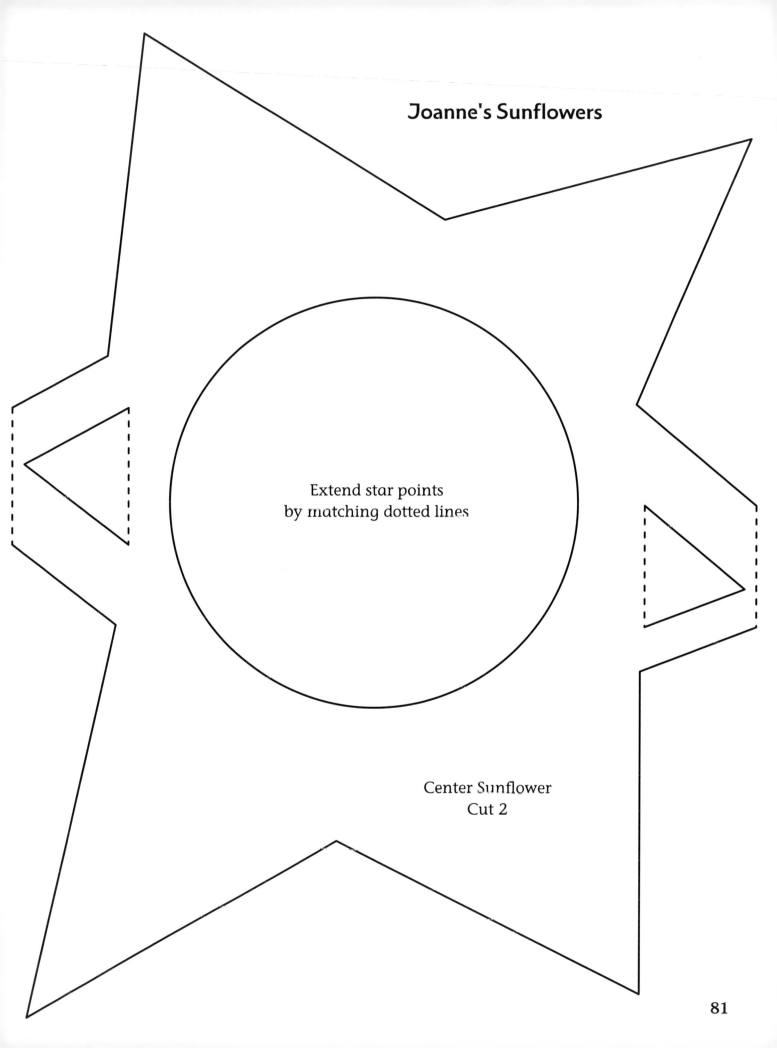

Joanne's Sunflowers

Extend star points
by matching dotted lines

Center Sunflower
Cut 2

Mad for Plaid Topper

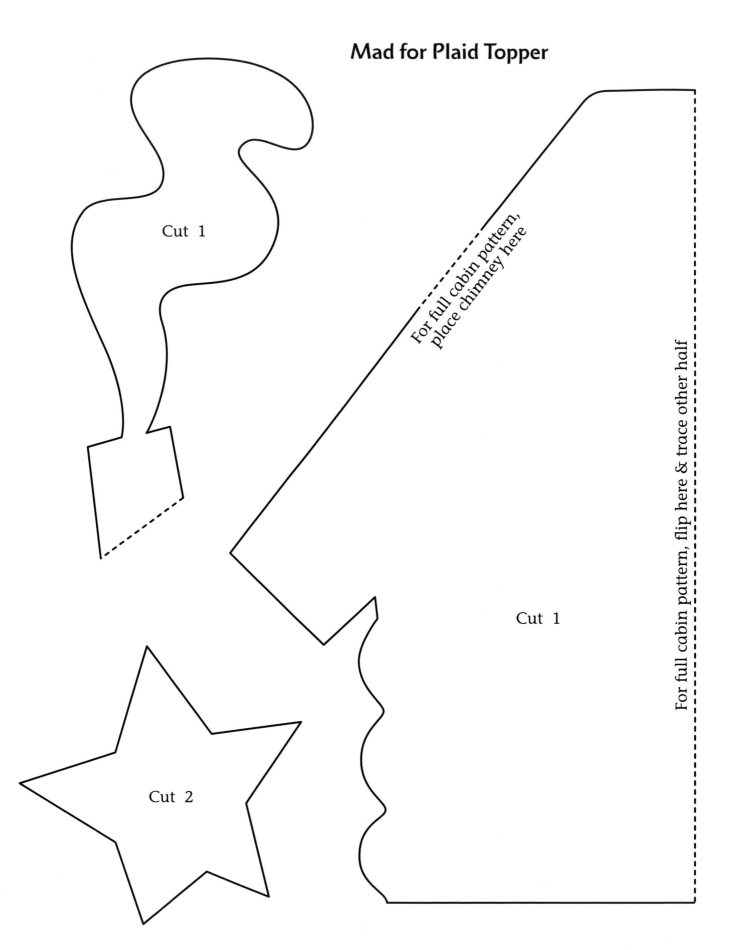

Cut 1

For full cabin pattern, place chimney here

Cut 1

For full cabin pattern, flip here & trace other half

Cut 2

82

Mad for Plaid Topper

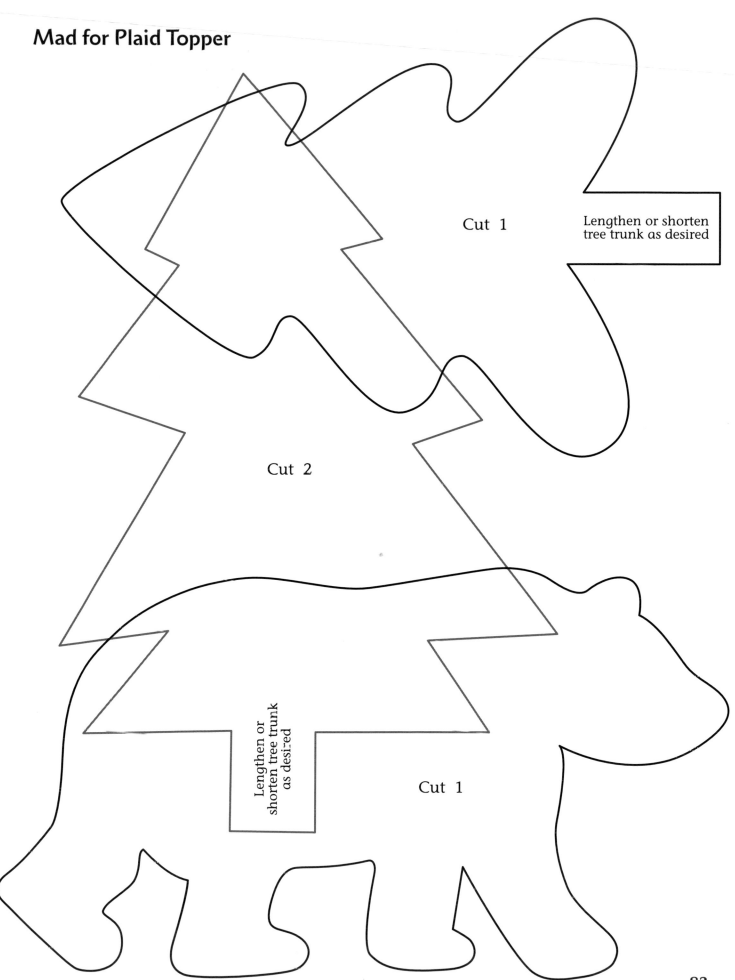

Cut 1

Lengthen or shorten
tree trunk as desired

Cut 2

Lengthen or
shorten tree trunk
as desired

Cut 1

83

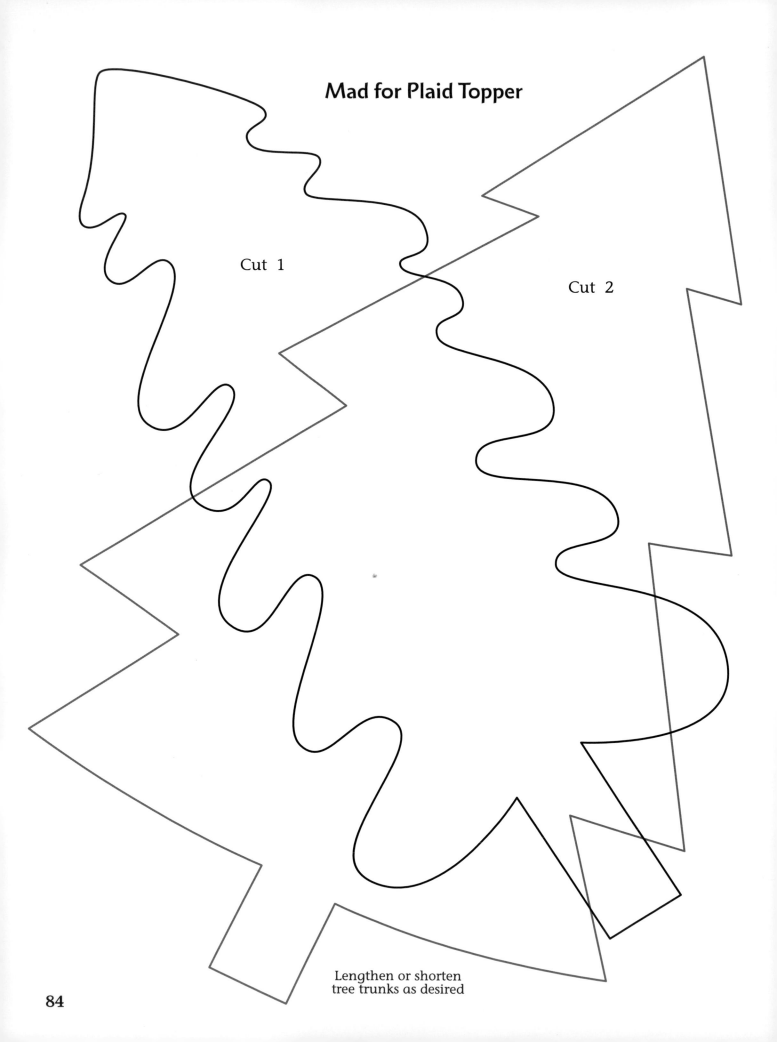

Mad for Plaid Topper

Cut 1

Cut 2

Lengthen or shorten
tree trunks as desired

84

Mad for Plaid Topper

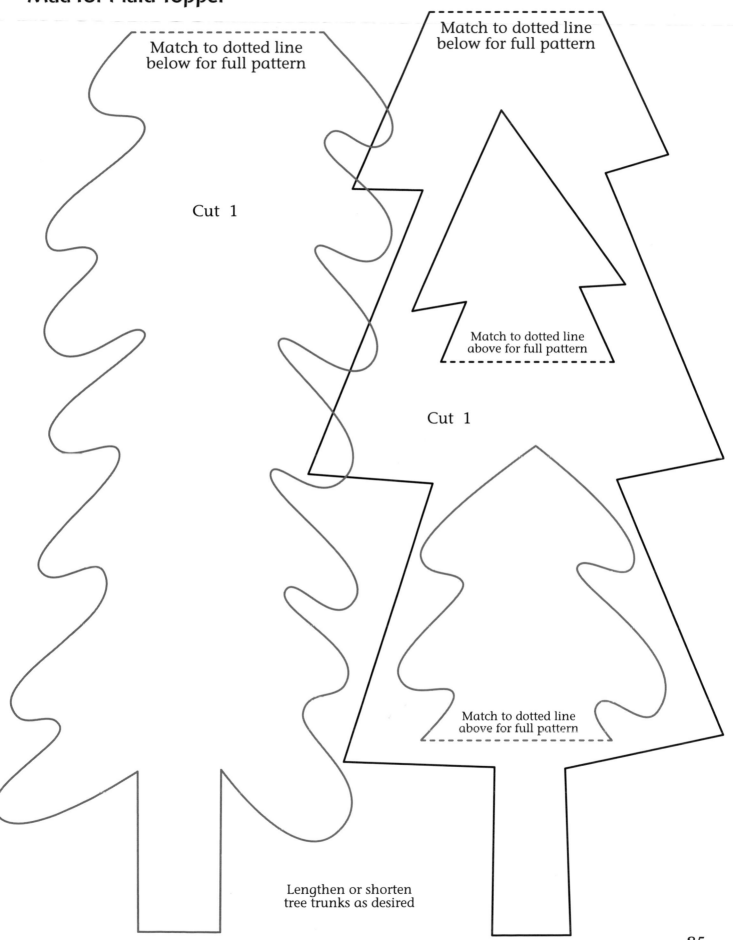

Match to dotted line
below for full pattern

Cut 1

Match to dotted line
below for full pattern

Match to dotted line
above for full pattern

Cut 1

Match to dotted line
above for full pattern

Lengthen or shorten
tree trunks as desired

Mad for Plaid Topper

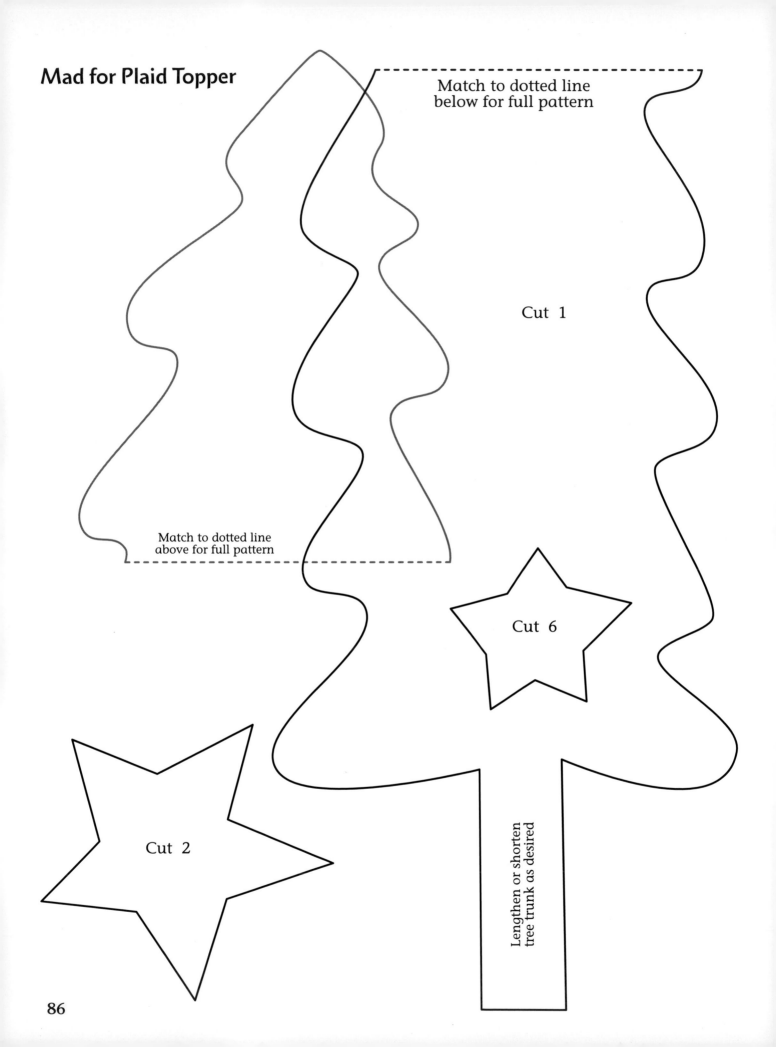

Match to dotted line
below for full pattern

Cut 1

Match to dotted line
above for full pattern

Cut 6

Cut 2

Lengthen or shorten
tree trunk as desired

Mediterranean Tiles

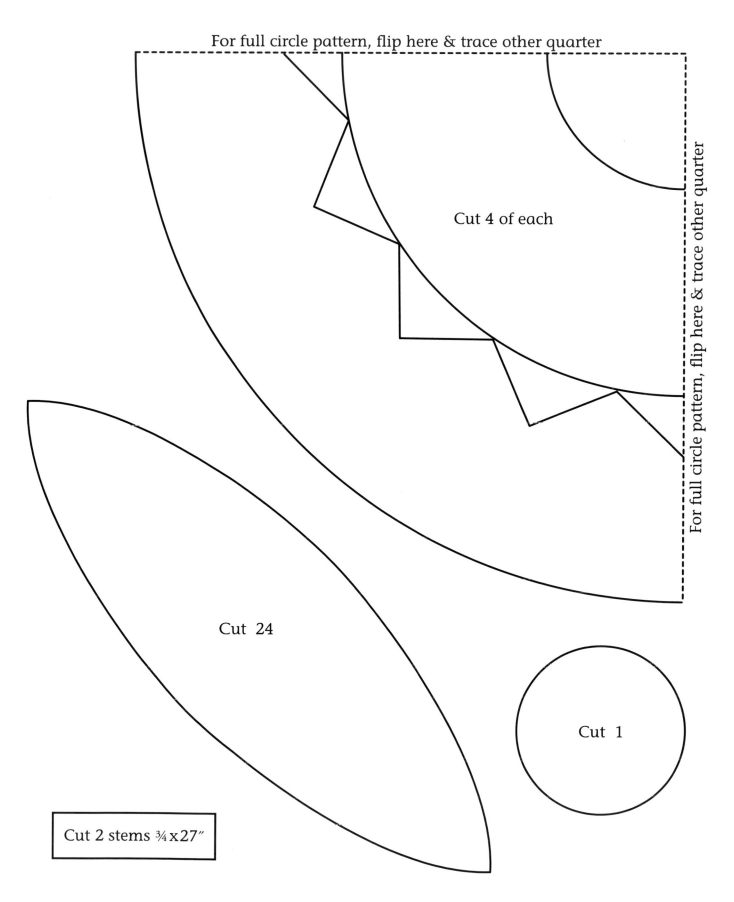

For full circle pattern, flip here & trace other quarter

Cut 4 of each

For full circle pattern, flip here & trace other quarter

Cut 24

Cut 1

Cut 2 stems ¾x27"

Creative Fabric Ideas from Possibilities®

Comforts of Love
Give the gift of love with one of six cozy patchwork and/or applique quilts. Coordinating pillow covers complete the look.

Home for the Harvest
Celebrate fall with 18 quilts and more than 20 small projects. Themes include back-to-school, Halloween, & Thanksgiving.

BedWarmers
Wrap your comforter in patchwork with one of three styles of comforter covers. Plus coordinated toppers, pillow covers, & pillow cases.

Cooking Possibilities
Over 100 recipes in this unique cookbook come from quilters across the country. Included are quilting hints & quilted projects for the kitchen.

Joy to the World
Full of holiday quilts for different skill levels. Contains delightful projects such as stockings, tree skirts, gift bags, and place mats.

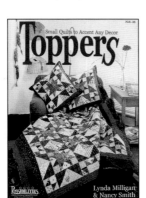

5 Easy Pieces
Use beautiful large florals to make custom decorator-style quilts & accessories. Large blocks & applique shapes.

Toppers
Toppers are beautiful quilts for displaying over bed pillows, on the back of a couch, or over a bedspread or comforter.

Quilts & More
Over 25 projects featuring photos transferred to fabric. Includes complete instructions and full-sized patterns for making family heirlooms.

HouseWarmers
Warm your home with the beauty of homemade quilts. Add personal touches to any room in the house. Nineteen quilts & 25 smaller projects.

Time for a Chain
Detailed charts for rotary cutting give measurements for single, double, and triple Irish Chains in two or three block sizes each.

P.S. I Love You
One of the top quilting books in America. Includes 17 quilts in cradle, crib, and twin sizes. Nursery accessories included. Exceptional collection!

POSSIBILITIES®
…Publishers of DreamSpinners® patterns, I'll Teach Myself™ sewing products, and Possibilities® books…

These books are available from your local quilt shop or from Possibilities® at:

8970 East Hampden Avenue
Denver, Colorado 80231

Phone 303-740-6206 • Fax 303-220-7424
Orders only U.S. & Canada 1-800-474-2665
Order online at www.possibilitiesquilt.com

P.S. I Love You Two!
A national top seller, this book features timeless projects for making cherished gifts for babies and children. A multitude of techniques is included.